New Teacher Mentoring

New Teacher Mentoring

Hopes and Promise for Improving Teacher Effectiveness

ELLEN MOIR, DARA BARLIN, JANET GLESS, AND JAN MILES

HARVARD EDUCATION PRESS
CAMBRIDGE, MASSACHUSETTS

Library of Congress Control Number 2009931671

Paperback ISBN 978-1-934742-36-5

Library Edition ISBN 978-1-934742-37-2

Published by Harvard Education Press,
an imprint of the Harvard Education Publishing Group

Harvard Education Press
8 Story Street
Cambridge, MA 02138

Cover Design: Sarah Henderson

The typefaces used in this book are Adobe Garamond Pro and Futura.

Contents

Acknowledgments

This book would not have been possible without the ongoing support and encouragement of a number of education leaders. In each of the districts we studied, district stakeholders provided full access to our researchers, allowing us to explore all elements of their mentoring programs and district policies. These stakeholders have been open and candid participants, willing to share the challenges, as well as the successes, of their efforts to support new teachers. Their willingness to disclose this data is testimony to their visionary leadership and their desire to prioritize deep learning, collaboration, and transparency over all else. We are confident that the this book project will yield great learning for teachers and students throughout the districts we studied, as well as districts around the country that are considering a transformation of mentoring programs.

Special thanks go to the following. From the Chicago Public Schools, Arne Duncan, U.S. secretary of education, former chief executive officer, Chicago Public Schools; Barbara Eason-Watkins, chief education officer; Xavier Botana, chief officer, instructional design and assessment; Lisa Vahey, former director, Chicago New Teacher Center; Cynthia Brunswick, director, Chicago New Teacher Center; and all principals, coaches, mentors, and new teachers who participated in the case study.

From the Durham Public Schools, Carl E. Harris, superintendent; Ann Denlinger, former superintendent; Fred Williams, executive director of recruitment and retention; Andrew Sieberg, former mentor; and all principals, coaches, mentors, and new teachers who participated in the case study.

From the New York City Department of Education, Joel Klein, chancellor; Amy McIntosh, chief talent officer; Audra Watson, executive director of teacher development; Randi Weingarten, president, United Federation of Teachers and American Federation of Teachers; Aminda Gentile, director, United Federation of Teachers' Teacher Center; and all former New York City mentors, regional directors, and UFT liaisons as well as the many LIMs, principals, APs, coaches, mentors, and new teachers who participated in the research project.

From the Boston Public Schools, Carol R. Johnson, superintendent; Kenneth Salim, director, new teacher development; Victoria Hom, senior program manager, new teacher development; and Richard Stutman, president, Boston Teachers Union.

From the Boston Plan for Excellence, Ellen Guiney, executive director; Jennifer Amigone, director of data analysis and evaluation; Ila Deshmukh Towery, director of policy analysis and research; Jesse Solomon, founding director of Boston Teacher Residency Program; and all principals, new teacher developers, and new teachers who participated in the case study.

Additional thanks go to Stacey Halls and Mel Barlin for their feedback, support, and ongoing encouragement during the writing process.

Introduction

The educational landscape in the United States is shifting. As more politicians call for reform efforts that are proven to improve student outcomes, a discourse has developed about how policy makers and school district leaders can impact the single most critical school-related variable in a child's education: the quality of the teacher. An awareness has emerged that a focus on new teachers represents powerful leverage for increasing teacher, and teaching, quality throughout the system.

From President Barack Obama, who has made support for new teachers a major pillar of his educational platform, to former governor Sarah Palin, who made new teacher mentor programs a top priority in Alaska's educational agenda, the message is clear and consistent (and apparently nonpartisan): a focus on support for new teachers can radically transform our schools.

The theory of change is simple. Research is clear that new teachers, because of their lack of experience and underdeveloped skills, are the least likely to help students achieve their academic potential. Yet school districts, especially in urban settings with high levels of attrition, have disproportionately large numbers of new teachers; up to 50 percent of teachers with less than five years' experience is not uncommon. By supporting new teachers and raising their level of effectiveness early in their careers, school districts therefore can dramatically improve student outcomes across the board.

Moreover, a focus on new teachers can begin to address the persistent student achievement gap, which has had powerful resilience in our nation's schools. The students who struggle most with education (generally low-income students of color whose parents have a limited or challenging history with formal education) are the most likely to be assigned to a classroom with an inexperienced teacher. This creates a cycle of inequity that sets up kids and teachers for failure. Concerted efforts to help new teachers become more effective earlier in their careers provide an opportunity to break the cycle and give those children who are most in need of a high-quality education a real chance at success.

The momentum behind this theory of change has spurred a race to figure out how to support new teachers in meaningful ways that manifest in growth for students. A slew of innovative initiatives has begun to be launched (or at least begun to be noticed) on the national stage. New performance pay schemes, alternative recruitment programs, sign-on bonuses, and tenure reform are only a few of the strategies being considered in districts, states, and at the federal level.

These initiatives generally seek to create incentives to improve recruitment or advancement of the most promising new teachers. The underlying philosophy of such incentive-based approaches is that the skills and knowledge to succeed already exist in some teachers and that they will come to the surface when bonuses are provided. These are important efforts that, especially in concert, will likely yield an improvement in the quality of teacher candidates in many settings. However, because these initiatives deal with incentives to identify some teachers (who already demonstrate exceptional skills) rather than develop the capacity of all teachers, the ability of these programs to affect the new teacher population as a whole— and at scale—remains limited.

Instructionally intensive, high-quality mentoring programs have risen to the surface as a promising strategy to support new teacher development, because these represent perhaps the only efforts designed to work with new teachers, who currently populate the majority of classrooms in our nation (regardless of the route they've taken to get there). The goal is to provide novice teachers with the tools they need to become excellent teachers. The underlying philosophy is that when new teachers don't achieve at high levels, it is not because they aren't trying hard enough nor because they don't care about the kids. Rather, it's that they don't yet have the skills or knowledge to provide the deep, complex level of instruction that will engage, motivate, and inspire their students to succeed.

The evidence is still in its nascent stages. But a number of indicators (described in chapter 1) suggest that when instructionally intensive mentoring programs are implemented well, when mentors help new teachers develop their skills in reaching the hearts and minds of the students in their classroom, new teachers want to remain in the classroom longer and are better able to help children, especially the most underserved kids, succeed at levels that defy expectations.

However, not all mentoring programs are built alike. The type of programs that have a meaningful impact on a new teacher's practice look much different from the traditional "buddy systems" or "mentor lite" programs that provide moral and logistical support alone. Although these programs have a place in making new teachers feel emotionally supported, they do little to build the capacity of the new teacher to impact the outcomes of kids. An instructionally focused program of support is needed if mentors are to impact new teacher behaviors and practice in meaningful ways that will eventually lead to better opportunities for students.

The New Teacher Center (NTC) has been providing instructionally intensive, high-quality mentoring support to first- and second-year teachers for more than two decades. We have served more than forty-nine thousand teachers, five thousand mentors, and millions of students in more than forty states, and we have participated in nearly thirteen hundred contracts with more than three hundred school districts in the United States and several countries around the globe. More recently we have begun to provide mentoring support to new principals and district leaders—critical stakeholders in supporting the growth of new teachers.

Although the NTC generally advocates for a specific model (including full-time release for mentors and comprehensive mentor training based on the NTC curriculum), our efforts in this book seek to move away from any one model and focus on the principles that underlie the most critical components of mentoring. These principles can be applied in any setting, from district programs and university clinical supervision models to union-led assistance initiatives and regional or cross-district collaborations. The structure and governance of mentoring programs can vary as widely as the teachers they seek to serve. The extent to which programs implement the principles of high-quality mentoring, and how well, dictates whether the programs will lead to better outcomes for kids or will be a waste of money with little or no impact on student or teacher success.

The first segment of this book—part I—therefore seeks to convey an understanding of what the principles of instructionally intensive, high-quality mentoring look like, along with a description of the potential impact that can be achieved. Chapter 1 provides an overview of what the research currently suggests (and doesn't) about the power of well-designed mentoring programs to impact teacher and student outcomes. It sets the stage for educational leaders who are considering investing in mentoring programs, with the goal of helping them understand what we currently know and don't know about impact. Chapter 2 describes the principles of high-quality mentoring, with a focus on those elements we believe to have the most potential to lead to improved practice. This chapter seeks to support educational leaders in understanding how to move away from traditional practices and toward robust, instructionally focused programs.

Chapter 3 focuses on one of the elements within these principles where NTC has the most expertise: mentor training. In this chapter, we explore NTC theories and philosophies that support a rigorous program of professional development that builds each mentor's complex and nuanced skill in moving new teachers' instructional practice forward. Together, these chapters seek to provide state, district, and program leaders with the knowledge they need to create comprehensive support for new teachers and ultimately to leverage instructional progress in the areas most in need.

With this background in mind, part II uses a case-study approach to explore the challenges of implementing high-quality mentoring programs. District and program leaders who envision even the most robust programs are sometimes derailed in implementation by circumstances beyond their control, especially in large urban settings. Superintendent turnover, well-entrenched (sometimes dysfunctional) practices and cultural norms, competing initiatives, limited communication structures, antiquated data systems, internal politics, a lack of institutional buy in, and a plethora of other factors can inhibit the most ambitious leaders from achieving successful implementation—especially in the early years of a program.

Added together, these contextual issues form a set of systemic obstacles that have added complexity to—and, at times, inhibited—efforts to put high-quality mentoring programs on the ground in large urban settings. The work has been exhilarating and thought provoking, both frustrating and rewarding. In some places we and our district partners have had banner-worthy success; in other places there have been bumps and bruises and lost opportunities. There is no doubt, however, that in all places we have developed insights into the process of reform (focused, in our case, on teacher mentoring) that have helped us, and the programs we work with, get better at doing the work.

Part II therefore focuses on the complexities of implementation and looks to unpack the nuanced relationship between high-quality, comprehensive mentoring programs and the cultural norms, practices, and structures of urban school systems. These relationships echo many of the NTC's experiences working with major urban districts around the United States and reflects the wide range of ways districts have interpreted and approached the principles of mentoring.

The presentation of these four case studies allows us to explore, in a deep way, critical strategies for implementing high-quality mentoring programs, the systemic obstacles we have seen emerge, and the innovative, politically savvy strategies that promise to overcome them. We recognize that these critical insights may not only be valuable to those seeking to support high-quality mentoring but may also apply to those seeking to foster change in school systems at any level.

We use a case-study approach in this book, in part, because it mirrors the methodologies we use with mentors and teachers to support ongoing learning and development. Our mentoring tools and protocols encourage mentors to invite their new teachers to focus on a single "case student" to better understand how to analyze students' specific learning needs and then to draw applications from that case of practice to the learning needs of other children. Similarly, our NTC mentor professional development protocols invoke a case approach to mentor learning by including recursive opportunities to review a single beginning teachers' case and apply the learning to all the new teachers each mentor supports.

In this vein, we seek to explore case studies at a systems level that invites readers to take a deep dive into a small number of district programs and then extrapolate issues, promising practices, and opportunities broadly to other contexts. By writing this book, we, too, have gained insights from these four cases of NTC practice and are seeking ways to apply that learning to the improvement of the center's work.

The heart of part II of this book focuses on the case studies found in chapters 4 through 7, where we focus on a subset of four urban district mentor programs: Durham, Boston, New York City, and Chicago. We delve deeply into those four cases to uncover the unique contextual factors, dilemmas, successes, critical strategies, solutions, and structures that characterize these mentoring reform efforts, as well as the NTC role in each setting. A number of interesting questions and challenges emerge from these cases, with powerful implications for future program and district practices.

For example, Durham challenges us to question whether the quality of the mentor can transcend the need for subject-matter matching, and whether using student test scores is an appropriate method for identifying potential mentors. In Boston we explore the trade-offs between part-time and full-time mentor release models and the nuances of supporting alternatively certified teachers (in this case through the Boston Teacher Residency program). New York City helps us think about new models of mentoring, the role of the mentor in school change, and ways to foster institutional buy in of a common vision of high-quality teaching. Chicago encourages us to explore how to create true alignment of instructional strategies across a system and how to provide meaningful support for principals in ways that foster significant teacher growth.

Each of these chapters highlights the trends and opportunities that we believe will have most resonance with other districts seeking to design or develop their own mentoring programs. Part III, composed of chapters 8 and 9, offers a bird's-eye perspective, reviewing the patterns that have emerged in multiple settings and providing recommendations for using these insights as guideposts for supporting program design and implementation in any context.

As a learning organization, the New Teacher Center is committed to reflecting on and integrating our evolving knowledge into our regular practice, and an important piece of that process involves making our work transparent. Just as we ask new teachers to open up their practice to mentors and principals, to be vulnerable and display both successes and challenges for shared learning and individual growth, we strive for the same degree of transparency by sharing our experiences and the lessons learned. The hope is that these insights will support better opportunities for teachers and students in all school systems.

We are indebted to the district leaders who were brave enough to join us in this endeavor. The Durham, Boston, New York, and Chicago mentoring programs represent some of the most powerful and cutting-edge models in the country. These district leaders' willingness to participate in this case-study process is testimony to their commitment to engage in deep learning about the program, to be transparent in their work, and to identify opportunities to help their new teachers thrive within and beyond their own districts. We are grateful for their vision, leadership, selflessness, and courage to articulate the challenges, as well as the successes, of their efforts.

In a recent speech to the National School Boards Association, U.S. Secretary of Education Arne Duncan called on the nation's education community to be more open about the work of education reform, asking us to disclose "the good, the bad and the ugly." The secretary's sentiment suggests that the United States can no longer afford to hide the challenges in the work, nor to be clandestine about key lessons that may help others do the work better.

The road to excellence in our schools is not smooth. On the contrary, it is long and fraught with potholes, speed bumps, fallen trees, and wrong turns. But if we are to truly transform our schools in meaningful ways, if we are finally to give children, all children, a chance for a great education, then efforts such as this book, and the leaders who have chosen to participate, may help pave the way toward success. So fasten your seatbelts. It's gonna be a bumpy—and educational—ride.

PART I

High-Quality
New Teacher
Mentoring

1

What We Know and Don't Know
About Mentoring and Induction

Over the past decade, a clear consensus has emerged that teacher quality is the most important school-related factor in student outcomes.[1] It dwarfs every other school-related variable with regard to academic performance, including class size, school size, and even the heterogeneity of prior achievement within a classroom.[2] Recent evidence highlights the cumulative impact of individual teachers on student performance. One study, which represented a collaborative effort of highly regarded researchers in the field, showed that poor and minority students who have an effective teacher four years in a row can achieve at the same levels as their more affluent white peers, thus potentially eliminating the student achievement gap.[3]

These findings suggest a powerful strategy for solving inequity in the U.S. public schools. If we can provide all children with consistent access to high-quality teachers, we can close the achievement gap and ensure that all students receive an excellent education regardless of race, background, or socioeconomic status.

The Council of Great City Schools (an association representing large U.S. urban school districts) reports, "More than any single approach, increasing the presence of effective, experienced teachers in schools and school districts serving poor and minority children represents the greatest single opportunity for reducing 'achievement gaps' and enabling our education system to provide all children with the education they need."[4]

Increasing the quality of teachers may be a powerful strategy for improving public education, but unfortunately we have yet to identify a strategy for overcoming the historical, logistical, and political roadblocks to implementing such a strategy. Low-income students and students of color throughout the United States continue to have limited access to high-quality teachers. Some research suggests that many teachers opt to leave inner-city schools for less-diverse settings where students experience higher levels of achievement. A recent survey of thousands of teachers showed that almost a quarter of new teachers felt they did not have adequate training for working with ethnically diverse student populations.[5]

A number of research studies have found that with regard to nearly every factor correlated with teacher quality, students from disadvantaged backgrounds get the short end of the stick. Children who are most in need of a high-quality education are the most likely to be assigned to classrooms where teachers are not certified in the subject they are teaching, failed their certification exams, came from the least competitive undergraduate institutions, or performed poorly in prior academic settings.[6]

Other studies suggest that teachers foster the lowest gains in student achievement in their first three years on the job, and yet students from high-poverty schools are nearly twice as likely to be assigned to new teachers as students from low-poverty schools.[7] This de facto assignment policy means that our most underprivileged populations, low-income students, and students of color receive new and inexperienced teachers year after year.

Perhaps more than any other, this trend perpetuates gaps in both teacher quality and student achievement. When the students most in need of a high-quality education are consistently placed in classrooms with the least experienced (and statistically least effective) teachers, school systems minimize the chance that these students will succeed in school and grow up to enjoy financially rewarding and meaningful employment. As demographics shift and as the percentage of students of color and English language learners continues to grow, the need to address this issue becomes even more pronounced. If nothing is done to reverse this trend, U.S. public schools will continue to replicate, and exacerbate, inequities within the larger society.

THE CONSEQUENCES OF NEW TEACHER ATTRITION

Policies to address the teacher quality gap must contend with a significant issue: many new teachers don't stay in the classroom long enough to become effective. About one-third of all teachers leave within their first three years on the job, and almost half leave within the first five years.[8] Attrition increases significantly in high-poverty and urban areas and is focused in critical subjects such as math, science, English language learning, and special education.[9] In many large urban school districts, more than half of the teacher population has less than five years' experience.[10] Additional studies have found dramatically low levels of teaching experience in a number of high-poverty settings.[11] This constant churning clearly has a negative impact on students and school communities.

As the National Commission on Teaching and America's Future points out, the teacher shortage crisis is like a "bucket with a fist-sized hole in the bottom." You can fill the bucket with water as much as you like, but as long as the water is rushing out almost as quickly as it is going in, you will never be able to fill the bucket. You must fix the hole. The teacher shortage is about not only recruitment but also retention.

Teacher attrition can also have an impact on school district budgets. One study explored the amount of lost funding by calculating recruitment efforts, teacher training, and other attrition costs related to new teacher turnover. The study determined that the United States as a whole loses approximately $7.3 billion annually.[12] The Alliance for Excellence in Education estimates losses at the state level; it calculates, for example, that in Illinois the loss amounts to approximately $224 million every year.[13] The impact becomes more pronounced at the local level when school district budgets are significantly affected. Teacher attrition costs an estimated $35 million annually in the Houston public schools, and nearly $115 million in New York City.[14] The Center for Strengthening the Teaching Profession finds that replacing every new teacher who leaves the profession costs $42,000 of taxpayer money.[15]

As with every profession, some level of attrition can be expected and is even positive if the teachers who leave are the least effective. Yet it appears that the most effective teachers are the first to leave. One study prepared for the U.S. Department of Education shows that teachers with the highest scores on certification tests are twice as likely to leave as those with the lowest scores.[16] A study conducted by the Urban Institute shows that as teachers working in the most challenging schools become more effective, they are more likely to leave.[17] Yet another study finds that fewer than 20 percent of teachers who are chosen through a highly selective alternative certification program are predicted to remain teaching in the nation's largest urban school district.[18]

These data points expose a systemic (and expensive) chasm in our education system that needs be addressed if we are to address teacher effectiveness in our schools. We must identify and implement policies that will keep our best and brightest teachers thriving and achieving in the classroom. The initial step in identifying which policies will be most successful in this endeavor is to understand why new teachers are leaving in such droves in the first place.

Why do new teachers leave?

Many surveys explore why so many new teachers leave the profession. Although salary is one of the reasons cited by teachers, other factors seem much more important. Studies from the U.S. Department of Education, the MetLife Foundation, and the New Teacher Center's (NTC) Teaching and Learning Conditions Survey suggest that the top factors influencing attrition include lack of support from school leadership, lack of empowerment, feelings of isolation or lack of relationships with colleagues, and undesirable teaching assignments.[19]

After digging deeper into these issues through extensive interviews with teachers who leave the profession, Susan Moore Johnson at Harvard University suggests that a teacher's sense of self-efficacy and the ability to reach the hearts and minds of students were pivotal to a teacher's decision to stay or leave teaching. Johnson writes, "Of central importance in all of the teachers' explanations of their decisions to stay in their schools, to move, or to leave teaching was whether they believed that they were achieving success with their students . . . If those teachers do not experience success with their students in the classroom, they are unlikely to stay."[20] Further evidence from NTC's statewide surveys on working conditions corroborates that finding: in the making future work plans, of paramount importance to teachers is their feeling of being effective with their students.[21]

The links between these studies are important. If the conditions of an educational community provide opportunities for new teachers to become effective (support from principal, instructionally intensive mentoring, developmentally appropriate assignments, etc.), then new teachers will feel more effective with their students and will want to remain teaching. If new teachers do not feel effective and if there are no structures in place to support them in becoming effective, they will likely seek employment elsewhere.

TEACHER MENTORING: LEVERAGE FOR ELIMINATING THE TEACHER QUALITY GAP

If a public school system is serious about achieving equity and ensuring that all students have access to an excellent education, it must confront the teacher quality gap. Aside from mandating the assignment of the best teachers to underachieving urban areas (an unpopular, politically divisive, and likely logistically impossible solution), we suggest two promising strategies for addressing this gap: (1) reducing the high rates of attrition among new teachers and (2) building the capacity of all new teachers to provide excellent instruction, thereby improving their effectiveness in helping students succeed from the first day they step into the classroom. High-quality mentoring—a term we use interchangeably with "instructionally intensive mentoring"— shows promise in achieving success with both of these strategies. Evidence has begun to accrue that shows high-quality mentoring programs, when implemented fully, can cut attrition rates, increase the effectiveness of new teachers, and even provide cost savings to schools and districts.

It is important to temper these promising ideas with caution about the evidence. There is no doubt that the research on high-quality mentoring is still in its nascent stages. Despite growing excitement and support for high-quality mentoring, there is a dearth of rigorous data. A few school districts have begun reporting publicly on new teacher outcomes, but the methods used to calculate these findings often are not transparent, and limited access to the data makes it difficult to formulate conclusive statements.

Empirical studies also leave room for improvement. In 2004, after conducting a meta-analysis of 150 empirical studies on mentoring, Richard Ingersoll found that only 10 met a standard of rigorous research. Of those, almost none was able to control for variables in addition to mentoring that might impact outcomes.[22] Only a few rigorous studies have been undertaken since this report.

To address this critical gap in data and open up the black box of mentoring, the New Teacher Center established the Research Division in its early stages of development. To ensure the credibility of the work, the directors created a firewall between the NTC and the Research Division. Except for consultation on the design of the research programs, all studies would be conducted by the division without the involvement of other departments within the NTC. With this firewall in place, the Research Division pursued myriad studies in California locations where it had most access to data and where there was funding to support research. Even with the firewall, however, the research has been housed within the scope of the New Teacher Center and therefore is subject to questions by external communities.

Additional independent studies have begun to emerge that are more rigorous, relative to historical research, and provide interesting insights on the impact of mentoring programs. However, the data is still limited in scope in many cases, and to be considered conclusive it needs to be augmented with research in larger settings.

More recently, districts have also begun to track better data on the impact of mentoring programs on teachers and students. It is important to note that school district reporting is not always as rigorous as that found in well-designed research studies. Many urban school districts have challenges collecting, analyzing, or reporting outcome data. Moreover, the task of reviewing retention data is not as straightforward as some might hope. Problems include disconnected data systems, lags in resignation processing, hiring discrepancies, inaccurate or inaccessible individual teacher identifiers, and even inadequate or inaccurate knowledge of teachers' locations. For logistical and political reasons, it is also difficult to collect student achievement data that can be disaggregated at the teacher level. In spite of these obstacles, some NTC partnership districts have managed to develop structures and procedures that capture the information on both teacher retention and gains in student achievement.

In the absence of a substantial body of evidence on mentoring, and with the foregoing caveats, we provide in the box "Recent Data on the Impact of

Mentoring" a review of a sampling of recent data that helps paint a picture of the impact of mentoring. In addition to a quick snapshot of the findings, the overview provides information about the location of the research and categories of research—whether the studies are independent, NTC initiated, or district based. Hopefully, this will allow readers to make their own determination about the conclusions that can be drawn.

Recent Data on the Impact of Mentoring

Site of Data Collection   Chicago Public Schools

Classification of Data   Independent research group

Conducted By   Chicago Consortium of School Research at the University of Chicago

Depending on school level, new teachers who receive strong mentoring and support (compared with those who receive weak mentoring and support) are three to four times as likely to say that they intend to remain at their school.

Site of Data Collection   Santa Cruz County Schools

Classification of Data   Non-independent research group

Conducted By   New Teacher Center Research Division

Two NTC studies looked at new teachers who participated in the Santa Cruz New Teacher Project mentoring program. The studies found that 88 percent remained in teaching after six years (compared with 56 percent after five years nationwide). These retention rates increase to 94 percent when teachers are included who move into school and district leadership positions.

An additional study conducted in one school district in Santa Cruz County with high levels of student poverty found that students in new teachers' classrooms performed on SAT9 achievement tests at virtually the same levels as students in veteran teachers' classrooms. Moreover, these students made these gains even though their classrooms had more English language learners, considered a traditionally harder-to-serve population. The novice teachers had received two years of instructional support from a carefully selected full-time mentor.

Site of Data Collection   NYC Department of Education

Classification of Data   Independent researcher

Conducted By   Jonah Rockoff, Columbia University Business School

The study found mixed results. There were substantial gains by students of new teachers in the program who had more time for interactions with their mentors. When new

---

(continued)

teachers spent more hours with their mentors (at least one hour per week, as reported by mentors), there were gains for students in both reading and math—especially math. The report suggests, "If truly causal, these effects would lend considerable support for the notion that mentoring has an impact on student achievement." The study also found that there was a positive impact on teacher retention when mentors had prior experience with and knowledge of a particular school. However, the mentoring program had no impact on retention and student learning overall across the system.[a]

Site of Data Collection Boston Public Schools

Classification of Data Non-independent research group

Conducted By New Teacher Center Research Division

A recent NTC study looked at differences in outcomes between two models implemented in the Boston public schools: (1) the use of fully released "new teacher developers" (the district's term for mentors) and (2) the use of site-based developers having full-time classroom duties. The study found that students whose teachers received support from full-release mentors showed better gains in achievement than did students associated with site-based mentors.

Site of Data Collection Durham Public Schools

Classification of Data School district reports

Conducted By Durham Public Schools

Durham Public Schools reports that the attrition rate of new teachers has been nearly halved since the start of its intensive mentoring initiative. The attrition rate before implementation of the program was nearly 30 percent, and the post-implementation attrition rate was less than 15 percent.

An internal review of student achievement gains compared initially licensed teachers (ILTs)—first-, second-, and third-year teachers participating in a mentor program—from multiple subject areas with veteran teachers who did not participate in the program. The report indicates that students of ILTs are making similar *or higher* gains in Algebra I, Geometry, Algebra II, English I, Biology, Chemistry, and Physical Science compared with students of their veteran peers.

Site of Data Collection Virginia Commonwealth University Program (review of three districts in consortium)

Classification of Data Independent research group[b]

Conducted By Virginia Commonwealth University

In one consortium district, first-year teachers were retained at a rate more than three times as great as the rate before implementation of the mentoring program.[c]

VCU also captured student test data from the Standards of Learning (SOL) tests administered in grades 3 through 8 by the state of Virginia. By comparing the test scores of students in new teachers' classrooms with those in veteran teachers' classrooms, VCU's study indicates that students of the new teachers in the mentoring pilot sites showed more than four times the gains of the comparison group.

Site of Data Collection   Ravenswood City School District

Classification of Data   Independent research group and non-independent

Conducted By   Center for Research on the Context of Teaching (Stanford University) and New Teacher Center

An intensified mentoring program (including additional elements focused on school improvement) started in Ravenswood in 2003–2004 at two schools. There was 75 percent attrition before the program was implemented, and 16 percent attrition two years after the program was implemented. From 2006–2007 to the present, the program has been expanded to all schools and has maintained approximately 80 percent retention (20 percent attrition) in all schools, including non-reelects.

Site of Data Collection   Chicago Public Schools

Classification of Data   Non-independent

Conducted By   Chicago New Teacher Center

CNTC has been tracking its own retention data, among other measures of success. In fall 2008, 85 percent of the first- and second-year teachers supported by CNTC returned to the district to teach. In addition, CNTC tracks "completion rates": the percentage of teachers who finish a school year. As of this writing, that rate is at 95 percent—this, in schools where vacancy rates traditionally topped 15 percent during the school year.[d]

Site of Data Collection   Alaska Statewide Mentoring Project (ASMP)[e]

Classification of Data   State-level reporting and independent researcher[f]

New teachers in Alaska are being retained at an average rate of 79 percent compared to a historic rate of 68 percent. First-year teachers in rural settings are being retained at a three-year average rate of 83 percent, compared with an average 67 percent retention rate for new teachers who are not in the program. In urban settings, new teachers are being retained at a three-year average rate of 94 percent; those who are not in the program are being retained at an average rate of 83 percent. A preliminary small-scale study in Alaska shows that new teachers in the mentor program are showing student gains on standardized assessments similar to those of more veteran peers.

Site of Data Collection   California Beginning Teacher Support and Assessment (BTSA) Program[g]

(continued)

Classification of Data   Independent research group

Conducted By   WestEd

Retention in the profession for both first- and second-year BTSA teachers is approximately 93 percent. During statewide expansion, the level of services remained the same or increased. The effectiveness of BTSA support is challenged by workplace conditions. BTSA has also had effects that reach beyond the program's main purpose of supporting beginning teachers. The organizational structures have helped teachers create intellectual communities that improve teacher practices as well as student achievement.

Site of Data Collection   Cost-benefit analysis based on NTC California partnership programs

Classification of Data   Non-independent

Conducted By   New Teacher Center Research Division

The study, validated by two external economists, measured the full range of benefits related to mentoring. It demonstrates a significant return on investment from expenditures on high-quality mentoring programs based on data from the Santa Cruz New Teacher Project. The study describes how each dollar invested in a comprehensive mentoring program provides a return on investment of $1.66 over five years. The analysis included all major and minor costs for providing high-quality new teacher support, including personnel, indirect costs (facilities, equipment, and materials), program inputs (such as room rental and substitute teachers), and client inputs (such as teachers' personal time). It also calculated the monetary benefit correlated with compensating new teachers who are equal to or more effective than their veteran peers.

The study concluded that high-quality mentoring programs provide a positive return on investment, both because beginning teachers stay in greater numbers and because those who stay are more effective. Benefits include potential savings to districts in increased teacher retention, increased new teacher effectiveness, and the time saved by principals through reduced need to monitor beginning teachers.

Site of Data Collection   Multi-City Pilot Initiative (Federal Study)

Classification of Data   Independent research groups

U.S. Dept. of Education, Institute of Education Sciences (IES), Mathematica Policy Research

This randomized controlled trial compared the implementation of a newly designed and implemented mentoring program—supported by NTC and Educational Testing Service—to a control group represented by the existing programs in seventeen urban school districts. The interim results from the first year of the multiyear study found that the program produced no significant impact on teacher retention, student achievement, or teaching practice. Results from additional years are pending.

[a]The data suggests that the power of mentoring can be realized when time for mentoring and alignment with school goals are in place. The lack of overall impact on teacher and student learning in New York City, however, suggests that these elements were not sufficiently present in most or all settings within the program. There are a number of potential reasons for this. The underlying issues stem from key obstacles to implementing all aspects of the work in the nation's largest urban school setting. This book seeks to uncover and explore those issues in detail.

[b]Research methods within the university are strong; however, the N is small.

[c]Although other factors may have contributed to this trend, a look at attrition across the pilot schools (with negligible differences in retention from the baseline to the pilot year) provides some support for the hypothesis that the mentoring program was a significant contributing factor in the increased retention.

[d]Comparable retention or completion data is not available for CPS, but the district has been pleased with these strong results. CNTC is continuing to expand its ability to collect, analyze, and report on important data on retention, teacher demographics, teacher development, and, eventually, student learning.

[e]The ASMP is a comprehensive, full-release program providing support for a subset of new teachers. The project is standards driven, employs NTC professional development for mentors, and follows formative assessment protocols (as defined in chapter 2).

[f]The achievement study methods are strong; however, there is a small N, and that makes results less generalizable. The state is currently funding the expansion of the study.

[g]N. Tushnett and Danielle Briggs, *Final Report of the Independent Evaluation of the Beginning Teacher Support and Assessment* [BSTA] *Program* (San Francisco: WestEd, April 2002), http://www.ctc.ca.gov/reports/BTSA-Eval-2003-Complete.pdf.

DISCUSSION OF THE IES–MATHEMATICA STUDY

In October 2008 the U.S. Department of Education's Institute of Education Sciences (IES), along with Mathematica Policy Research, Inc., released the initial first-year results of a multiyear study on comprehensive teacher mentoring.[23] This randomized controlled trial compared the implementation of a newly designed and implemented mentoring program (treatment)—supported by NTC and Educational Testing Service—to a control group represented by the existing programs in seventeen urban school districts.

This study represents the largest quantitative research effort to date to understand the impact of mentoring programs. The level of investment in this high-intensity effort reflects significant growth in the interest in mentoring and induction in the United States. The study negotiated and implemented a randomized controlled study—one that was conducted in more than a dozen districts and controlled for a multitude of school, district, and contextual factors. The study's first interim report did not include a significant qualitative component. NTC entered into this study to contribute to the nascent research in the field of mentoring and to be a part of the effort to identify how, and to what extent, mentoring can impact teachers' and students' lives.

The interim results from the first year of this multiyear study found that the program produced no significant impact on teacher retention, student achievement, or teaching practice.

These interim results were disappointing, because they countered much of the emerging, more promising data on mentoring that was beginning to accrue. The methodology and the level of investment in the intensity of the research led many to question why no impact was found. A review of the research design and implementation raises important questions about qualitative aspects of the study.

Qualitative aspects of the study

The first question reflects the modified design of the programs in the study. For experimental purposes, the research design modified the NTC's typical mentoring program. As the authors note, "The study was intended to explore the effects of comprehensive teacher induction in general, not the specific impacts of any one program." The studied programs did not include many of the elements that are found in robust NTC programs. NTC understood this entering into the study but felt that this approach to new teacher support was worth testing. However, some of the elements omitted from the design might have implications for the impact of the work on teachers and students.

Following are some of the elements that were not included in the study.

- *Participation by a variety of key stakeholder groups:* In fully implemented NTC programs, leaders from throughout the district community (i.e., the superintendent's office, teachers union, office of human resources, universities, department of teaching and learning, etc.) come together to align the strategies for supporting new teachers and building a common vision for high-quality instruction.

- *Engaging site administrators:* Typical NTC programs engage in a series of activities or aggressive strategies to engage site administrators in the program and provide additional resources to support princi-pals in building effective communities for new teachers. Examples of such strategies are described in the case studies in this book. The pro-grams in the IES–Mathematica study were limited to the provision of occasional administrator information sessions, which often were not widely attended. No additional activities took place. As a result, as the study reports, "Schools and districts evidenced wide variation in the level of principal support, ranging from principals who were extremely supportive to principals who actively resisted participation and would not permit teachers to be released for program activities."

- *Links to schools of education (pre-service):* NTC's most promising pro-grams create a seamless transition between, on the one hand, theory learned in university schools of education before teachers enter the profession and, on the other hand, the application of that theory in the classroom when they enter their schools for the first time as teach-ers. The study's design did not allow for the long-term relationship building necessary to create these links.

The second question focuses on the quality and consistency of the im-plementation of the mentoring programs. Some bumps in the road are inevitable in the first year of any new program. Typically, programs have the opportunity to work out implementation kinks in the second year and beyond. Because the study required that the implementation of each pro-gram occur in the same year as the evaluation of the program, it may have adversely impacted the results.

Three possible concerns about implementation are described here.

- *Mentor recruitment and selection:* The most important element of any mentoring program is the quality of the mentor. To be successful, dis-tricts must recruit and select talented educators who also demonstrate a particular set of dispositions and skills (mastery of content and ped-agogy, strong interpersonal skills, knowledge of adult learners, ability to collaborate, and so on).

  Mentors in the study were selected extremely late (in August, in some cases), when many educators had already committed to teaching and other leadership roles. In many districts the mentor recruitment effort was limited, with little information articulated about the scope or importance of the work. The combination of a condensed implementation schedule and scant information meant that many top educators were unavailable, unaware, or uninterested in applying for the positions. As a result, the applicant pool for the position of mentors in some of the programs was inadequate.

- *Mentor experience:* All the educators who were being selected to be first-year mentors were being trained as the program was being implemented. By December, the mentors had received only half their training, which continued through May. Few mechanisms were provided to help these mentors accelerate their steep learning curve. In comparison, programs that have been in place for at least three years provide support (such as pairing with more senior mentors and one-on-one coaching from experienced program directors) to help bring first-year mentors up to speed.

- *Program leadership:* The program did not offer full-time mentoring program leaders to support the work of the mentors and thus lacked a typical element of NTC's full model. A program coordinator was identified at each site, but as the IES–Mathematica report notes, "Given that the coordinator role was an addition to a full set of existing responsibilities, coordinators struggled to carve out the time needed for program implementation."

The third question concerns the level of difference between the program and the control group; the programs being implemented for the study (treatment group) may not have been significantly different from the existing mentoring model experienced by new teachers in the control group. Such a similarity between groups can lead to what researchers call a type II error (a false negative).[24] For example, in this study, the amount of time that new teachers spent with their mentors differed by only twenty-one minutes per week; new teachers in the control group received more than sixty minutes per week with their mentors, and those in the study group received eighty-one minutes. NTC mentoring implementation rubrics suggest that more than sixty minutes per week with a new teacher constitutes a relatively robust program compared with many typical programs, in which new teachers meet ten to thirty minutes per week or less.

This intensive level of support is unusual and invites questions about the intensity of mentoring programs in the control group—whether they represented typical programs or uncharacteristically above-average programs incorporating many of the principles of high-quality mentoring. A challenge in more deeply analyzing the differences between the control and study groups is the lack of available information about the nature of mentoring programs in the control group, including the qualifications, training, and years of experience of the control-group mentors. The researchers of the study suggest this information was not collected, making a review of the comparison impossible.

Recent conversations have noted the challenges associated with randomized controlled studies when conducted in complex educational environments. A number of these recent studies conducted by IES have yielded limited or no effects, a trend that is "prompting researchers, product developers, and other experts to question the design of the studies, whether the methodology they use is suited to the messy real world of education."[25] Some of these studies have been criticized for the same, or similar, reasons as the problems associated with the mentoring study: insufficient differentiation between treatment and control groups and poor fidelity of implementation.

These questions do not represent a negation of the extensive efforts to assess the impact of the work. Rather, these questions represent important insights that may enable future researchers to collect data in ways that reflect the complex layers of education reform. To support future efforts, a number of recommendations have been provided below.

Recommendations

After assessing NTC's participation in a randomized controlled study, we have begun to identify opportunities to strengthen research efforts in the future to be more fully reflective of the work. First, NTC recommends incorporating a strong qualitative component in all research designs to allow for nuanced assessments of implementation. With this information in hand, researchers could conduct a treatment analysis to measure the impact of the work in places where implementation is high. An alternative approach would be to study programs that have been in existence for at least two years and show evidence of fully implementing all the key elements of mentoring.

Either way, such an effort would significantly provide program and district leaders with critical insights that would help to inform and support program development—a key missing ingredient in research efforts that do not incorporate qualitative data.

Second, researchers should seek to collect and provide information on induction programs at the school level (in addition to the district level). Many school district central offices may be unaware of the types and level of support provided to new teachers in the schools. There are myriad ways schools approach support for new teachers. When done well, these supports can be aligned with the principles of high-quality mentoring. Randomized controlled studies that seek to create control groups and treatment groups must look at these variables to ensure sufficient uniqueness of programs.

Finally, NTC recommends that future studies review the impact of the full NTC program or other high-quality induction programs incorporating the full range of elements, and review to what extent such factors (university participation, district alignment, roles for site-based administrators, and so on) may have an impact on the success of new teachers.[26]

IMPLICATIONS FOR RESEARCH

Research on mentoring is still in its infancy. Lack of access to data, small sample sizes, and high variation in data collection and reporting continue to plague the field. However, local program data, coupled with emerging research studies, suggests that mentoring may have a positive impact on two important goals: increased teacher retention and accelerated new teacher development (leading to improved outcomes for students). Program data—including data collected by programs in Santa Cruz, Durham, and Alaska—suggest that with intensive mentoring support, new teachers in their first years can become as effective as, or even more effective than, their veteran peers. The additional benefit of cost savings to school systems may also be realized.

At the same time, additional research indicates that we cannot yet claim success. The IES–Mathematica study has raised new questions about the ability of mentoring programs to impact outcomes in the first year, and the New York City report leads us to ask what the barriers are to creating impact at scale. Importantly, in both of these studies, one of the primary questions that emerges concerns implementation. There are limits to officials' ability to implement high-quality mentoring (including critical elements such as time for interactions, mentor selection, principal engagement, and so on), and these limits may serve as significant and powerful barriers to realizing outcomes. Implementation—especially in large urban school districts—can be extremely tricky.

The following chapters discuss the principles of high-quality mentoring and explore how districts can navigate the bumpy road of implementation in order to realize the gains in teacher and student learning that can ultimately be made.

2
—

The Principles of High-Quality Mentoring

The term "teacher induction" conjures a variety of images. Some people hear the term and think of a well-planned, supportive orientation day. Others recall the hardships and frustrations that frame a teacher's first year on the job. Still others jump to the idea of a robust mentoring program. All these images fall within the larger scope of induction, but there is power in understanding a new teacher's transition into teaching within a defined framework that focuses on three features: (1) a phase of teacher development, (2) a period of socialization and enculturation, and (3) a formal program for beginning teachers.[1]

Induction represents one of the most critical periods in a teacher's career. During this *phase of teacher development,* teachers learn to apply the theory and knowledge acquired in pre-service to the day-to-day practice of teaching. It's a period of firsts, when novice teachers learn to solve problems, establish professional routines, deepen emerging skills, and develop the habits of mind necessary to become effective classroom educators.[2] It's also a time when beginning teachers, especially those under stress, are likely to revert to strategies and methodologies they experienced as students, regardless of the sound theories and practices introduced during pre-service education. For new teachers who enter the classroom without the benefit of teacher education experiences, these first two to three years are even more important as they simultaneously work to acquire both theory and practical knowledge while carrying a full-time teaching load.

Teachers may learn new teaching methods, styles, or strategies later in their careers, but the foundation—how they interact with students, what types of expectations they set, and whether their kids will be bored or inspired—is laid in the first couple of years on the job.

A teacher's induction is also a *period of socialization and enculturation,* a time when their professional attitudes and behaviors are shaped by the culture that exists within the school and district community. If new teachers are constantly exposed to other teachers and administrators talking down to students and bad-mouthing parents in the faculty lounge, most will eventually mimic those behaviors. It is difficult to resist this culture of negative attitudes, and chances are those attitudes will eventually seep in and alter teachers' perspectives as well as behaviors. Those who fight hard to maintain individual integrity when it conflicts with the school's culture often give up out of frustration. On the other hand, if a novice teacher's experience is steeped in a positive culture—where other teachers share instructional strategies, support one another, and exchange successful ways to reach out to and work with parents—these teachers will likely emulate a similar ethos and positivism.

The third aspect of induction, a *formal program for beginning teachers,* comes in many shapes and sizes. A formal induction program can mean a three-day orientation in which teachers sit passively through a series of speakers welcoming them and explaining the protocols of the school and district. Or it can mean a concerted effort to pair a new teacher with a veteran teacher to walk through the school's resources, administrative details, and bathroom locations. For districts that take a more comprehensive approach, a formal induction program might mean a multiyear, multipronged effort to provide new teachers with intensive instructional guidance, networking opportunities, and access to critical resources and conversations that support the transition into their new roles.

Regardless of the type of program, one thing is certain: the first two features of induction will occur whether or not a formal program is in place. New teachers will go through a period of development; and they will be encultured and socialized by the dominant practices and attitudes of their particular context, whether those features positively influence their teaching effectiveness—or not. If there is no support for new teachers and no structures in place to help them survive the bumpy transition into the classroom, new teachers will experience the common sink-or-swim model of induction—an isolating, frustrating experience in which teachers learn their craft by hook or by crook. Those who don't quickly learn to swim will be among the first to leave the profession.

By implementing a formal, high-quality, comprehensive induction program, school officials can influence both the new teacher's development and her socialization and enculturation. From the very beginning, such programs establish norms and practices that foster reflective practitioners who understand how to assess the needs of their students, tailor instruction based on those needs, and use data from the classroom to regularly, and rigorously, inform their own instructional practice. The benefits of such a program continue to accrue throughout all the years of a teacher's career.

DEFINING HIGH-QUALITY MENTORING

In chapter 1, numerous research studies are cited that suggest the potential impact of high-quality mentoring on teacher retention and student achievement. One study even highlights the cost savings to school districts that invest in rigorous new teacher programs. However, the research community is less clear about what constitutes high-quality mentoring.

One or two studies review outcomes related to easily identifiable components of induction programs.[3] Unfortunately, because research in induction and mentoring is still emerging, reviews must rely on instruments that incorporate limited or crude data. No research so far takes a comprehensive look at all induction elements and identifies which are the most critical for ensuring the success of new teachers. Thus districts interested in developing or enhancing programs have been left to intuit what effective induction programs might look like.

Unfortunately, not all elements of high-quality mentoring are intuitive. In fact, many of the elements challenge long-held assumptions and debunk well-entrenched practices in U.S. school systems. The principles of high-quality mentoring provide a platform for transforming these age-old practices and leveraging meaningful systemic change that matters for kids.

The following overview outlines the principles underlying the components of high-quality mentoring. Although these principles are at the heart of the New Teacher Center's typical model, they are not specific to NTC.

They can be applied in any school or district context, regardless of size, location, governance structure, or partnership support. The level of success for new teachers is not about who implements the principles but how they are implemented.

Note that each district faces trade-offs and variations as it implements mentoring programs under its particular circumstances. Stemming from NTC experience working with a range of districts, these guidelines articulate what is critical to program success in various contexts.

PRINCIPLE 1: RECRUIT, SELECT, TRAIN, AND SUPPORT HIGHLY SKILLED MENTORS

Much as the classroom teacher has been shown to be the single most important ingredient in student learning, the mentor is the most critical element in an effective mentoring program. No matter which model is used or which management structure is provided, if the mentors in a program are outstanding, the program will be outstanding and new teachers will have the opportunity to reflect meaningfully on their practice and accelerate their instructional growth. If the mentors are subpar, the program will be less effective and new teachers often will not get the resources they need to be successful in the classroom. If a mentoring program is to succeed, its first priority must be to ensure that it has identified and selected the most talented mentors to work with new teachers. The second priority is to build the capacity of those mentors so that they can be effective in their roles.

Mentor recruitment

Like teacher recruitment, mentor recruitment is a key step in building effective programs. There are two paths to excellence in recruitment. The first is to include all high-level stakeholders (those who make, or influence, critical decisions about teaching and learning) in a highly visible communication campaign that underscores the value and rigor of the new mentoring program. This high-level support builds support for the program, raises the prestige of the mentor position, and helps to secure a large, high-quality pool of applicants. The second path is to engage in a personalized effort to identify those who would make extraordinary mentor candidates and then woo these individuals through any means necessary. (Many top educators do not want to leave the classroom; these educators often make the best mentors.) Many effective programs engage in both approaches simultaneously.

Building the cachet associated with becoming a rigorously selected mentor is also critical, especially when programs are getting off the ground and the roles, responsibilities, and expectations for the mentors are not yet understood. If you do not make an energetic effort to clarify the new program's goals and recruit highly qualified individuals, the mentor pool may be slim. Or many potential candidates will assume that the program is simply another flavor-of-the-month initiative or another casual buddy system—and the pool of applicants will be of lower quality. For more information on successful recruitment efforts in urban settings, see chapters 5 and 7.

Mentor selection

Once a high-quality pool of applicants has been secured, programs must conduct a rigorous selection process. Many traditional selection routines identify and assign mentors based on who has time available to meet with the new teacher, who has the most seniority in the contract, or who has the closest relationship with the principal. These practices are logistically easy for school and district administrators, but they have the potential to perpetuate poor or mediocre teaching practice. A rigorous selection process prioritizes the attributes of a high-quality mentor over ease of schedule, contract provisions, or perks to specific teachers.

Although school districts may consider a host of attributes when searching for high-quality mentors, selection criteria should at least include the following:

- Evidence of outstanding teaching practice
- Strong interpersonal skills
- Experience with adult learners
- At least five years of teaching experience
- Respect of peers
- Current knowledge of curriculum and professional development
- History of advocacy leading to change
- Commitment to lifelong learning

A rigorous program also ensures that the process for selection is transparent, uses rubrics to standardize selection, and involves multiple key stakeholders. These elements support accountability for high selection standards, build commitment for the program, and, most importantly, help stakeholders generate a common framework for understanding how to identify and build human capital in schools. Wherever possible, the selection panels should include mentor program leaders, site and district administrators, union or teacher organization leaders, veteran teacher leaders, former or current mentors, university clinical and tenured faculty, and district leaders.

For more insights on mentor selection, see chapters 5 and 6.

Professional development of mentors

Although districts can spend much time and energy on identifying and hiring the most qualified mentor candidates, the job does not end there. Once hired, mentors must be trained in the art of guiding new teachers through their first years on the job. Without in-depth professional development, many mentors will revert to the "tell them what I know" strategy. This approach might feel nice for the mentor, who can impart some of the knowledge accrued over many years in schools, but it is not effective in building the capacity of the teacher to improve. Teachers improve most when their learning is self-directed, tailored to meet their own individual needs, and based on real-time data from their own instructional efforts.

Mentors must therefore develop an acute ability to collect and review data concerning a teacher's practice as well as possess sophisticated skills in sharing data in ways that build trust and encourage reflection and an instinct for asking questions. These capabilities support new teachers in developing the habits of mind that will help them become effective practitioners. Mentors must also have or develop a strong understanding of and ability to articulate what the elements of high-quality teaching and effective student learning look like in the classroom. Even master teachers, who don't always know what it is about their own teaching that is so effective, may find it challenging to acquire these abilities.

Being an effective mentor requires entirely new skills, and it takes time, sophisticated training, and ongoing coaching and reflection to develop them.

Rigorous and well-structured professional development is therefore critical in supporting mentors to become highly effective in their new role.

Ongoing support through a community of practice

Professional development should not be seen only as a training protocol. By implementing a rigorous, instructionally sound mentoring program, schools and districts develop a cadre of teacher leaders who will become catalysts for improving instruction throughout a school system. It is essential that these teacher leaders participate in a community where they deepen their understanding of this important work, collectively review data on new teachers, share best practices, and hone their mentoring skills.

The best way to create this community is to bring mentors together weekly or every other week with facilitators who can help structure conversations focused on moving teacher practice forward. Program leaders provide the type of support for mentors that mentors provide for new teachers and ultimately teachers provide for their students—a concept one New York City leader calls "cascades of consistency."[4] The support for mentors should therefore be tailored to their individual needs, focused on the use of data drawn from practice, and supported by ongoing coaching and feedback.

Additional information on effective mentor communities of practice can be found in chapter 5.

Mentor evaluation

Just like teachers, mentors need leaders who can optimize their growth. Program leaders must understand what high-quality mentoring interactions look like and must have the time to devote to shadowing, providing clear feedback based on data, and developing formal structures for evaluation. Program leaders should use rubrics and goal-setting protocols to ensure that mentors are continuing to grow in their practice. Survey data from teachers and administrators should also be triangulated with mentor perceptions about the program. This data helps build a realistic understanding of mentor effectiveness and creates a road map for professional development based on the individual mentor's strengths and challenges.

A three-year rotation for mentors

An important aspect of mentoring is having solid, current knowledge of classroom practice. Mentors who have not taught for many years may have a somewhat outdated knowledge of curricula and strategies and may be out of touch with current needs of classroom teachers. Recent classroom experience helps mentors support new teachers as they learn and practice instructional strategies currently being implemented by the district.

By implementing a three-year rotation, a program can infuse mentors with current knowledge and innovative classroom strategies. In this rotation, mentors come out of the classroom for three years to serve as mentors and then return to the classroom or move on to leadership positions.

A staggered rotation helps programs avoid losing the lion's share of their highly skilled mentors at any one time. This approach also ensures that the district has a cohort of mentor leaders to support the new mentors' development and has a cadre of new mentors to bring knowledge of the most recent instructional and curricular initiatives. Strong programs also capitalize on the talents of the strongest mentors, tapping them to serve in leadership roles and to innovate program design and implementation.

PRINCIPLE 2: SANCTION AND REINFORCE TIME FOR MEANINGFUL MENTORING INTERACTIONS

Finding and developing effective mentors are critical elements of successful mentoring programs. However, if school officials do not provide the conditions that support mentors having meaningful interactions with new teachers, mentors cannot achieve the goal of moving teacher practice forward.

Full or substantial release time for mentors

In some programs, meetings between mentors and new teachers occur occasionally or whenever the mentor and teacher are available. Both parties are often so busy with their own responsibilities that meeting time becomes a low priority. Even when some release time is provided, mentors are occasionally asked to take on other last-minute responsibilities (such as covering classes, proctoring exams, serving lunch duty, and doing paperwork), and the time for mentoring gets whittled down. If mentors do not have time to get into new teachers' classrooms to see their instructional practice in action, mentors' feedback will be underinformed and significantly less meaningful. Mentors need regularly protected time to observe, reflect on, and discuss the teacher's practice. Limited fragments of time between classes or "other duties as assigned" are not sufficient for fostering growth in beginning teachers.

Recent research shows the critical importance of reserving time for interaction in mentoring activities. One report indicates that interaction time between mentor and teacher has a substantial effect on teachers' abilities to impact student achievement gains.[5] NTC experience, coupled with this new research, suggests that mentors and new teachers need between 1.5 and 2.5 hours per week for interactions, whether the mentoring model is full-time or part-time release.

Sanctioning this time is much easier in a full-time release model in which mentors have no more than fifteen new teachers and work in no more than four schools. (NTC recommends lowering the full-time mentor caseload to seven to ten new teachers in the hardest-to-staff schools or in areas needing more intensive support.) Some research shows that full-time release mentoring (compared with part-time release models) has greater impact on student achievement and leads to increased feelings of support on the part of new teachers.[6]

The full-time release approach offers additional, less obvious advantages. Full-time mentors who work each year with as many as fifteen new teachers are likely to develop their mentoring knowledge and skills much faster than those who are balancing classroom teaching with mentoring duties and who may work with only one or two new teachers a year. Full-time mentors practice their mentoring day in and day out, observing and collecting data in dozens of classrooms and engaging in mentoring conversations every day, making this observation a matter of common sense.[7] It stands to reason, therefore, that full-time mentors may reach a peak level of effectiveness more quickly than their part-time counterparts.

Some part-time release programs create structures that set aside the appropriate time for meaningful interactions between new teachers and mentors. In these cases, district leaders engage in intensive, ongoing campaigns to ensure that site administrators understand the value of instructional mentoring and professional development and actively protect the allotted hours for interactions. This level of proactivity ensures that mentors are not pulled off task when other school priorities arise (a typical and dangerous practice that dilutes the impact of any program).

Multiyear mentoring

If the goal is to improve teacher practice and consequent student achievement, mentoring should be intensive and ongoing (for at least two years). One-year mentoring programs can provide the initial support first-year teachers need to survive but are not sufficient to help teachers reach optimal effectiveness.

According to Feiman-Nemser's NAEP review of the professional literature, a teacher's period of induction is variously described as lasting from three to five years. In addition, there is general consensus that teacher induction needs to be multiyear, because most deep learning about instruction (through mentoring) happens during the second and third years of teaching.[8] Therefore, the rigor and time committed to mentoring in a teacher's second year should be just as great as in the first year.

PRINCIPLE 3: FOCUS INTERACTIONS ON CLASSROOM AND STUDENT DATA

There is a significant and important difference between traditional mentoring and rigorous instructional mentoring. In the former, teachers may receive moral and logistical support that might feel good in the moment but by itself is not sufficient for improving teaching practice. Examples might be a mentor leaving a gift in the new teacher's mailbox or popping in during prep time every now and again to say, "You are doing a great job, Jane. Keep it up!" Without specific instructional feedback, mentoring might boost spirits for the short term, but it will not impact student learning.

Instructional mentoring ensures that all interactions are grounded in evidence and critical dialogues about instruction. Although a strong, trusting relationship is an essential component of an effective mentoring relationship, the focus of high-quality programs remains on advancing the beginning teacher's classroom practice. Mentors who are trained to draw upon professional teaching standards, formative assessments, and appropriate content-area standards focus their support on long-term instructional growth as well as concrete next steps to help new teachers improve their teaching.

An example from an instructional mentoring program might show a mentor coming into the classroom and suggesting to the new teacher, "Let's look at your student assessment data and talk about what strategies will help you address the concern you had about reaching your struggling English language learners."

Formative assessment and teaching standards

Just like student learning, new teacher learning should be data driven and standards based. Effective feedback for beginning teachers is grounded in evidence about their practice and includes information gathered through classroom observations and student work. Mentors collect information on teacher practice and then engage the new teacher in the collaborative analysis of the data and assessment of his instruction and student learning. This fully integrated formative assessment helps guide the beginning teacher's next steps, as well as the mentor's, and models the power of assessment for learning.

Professional teaching standards delineate the knowledge, skills, and dispositions that constitute highly effective teaching.[9] These standards serve as a common platform for mentors and new teachers as they collect and analyze data, set professional goals, and engage in instructional dialogues that set forth next steps. Mentors, new teachers, and administrators can link feedback on practice to a clearly articulated and commonly held set of desired teaching behaviors. Mentors can assist their teachers in determining instructional progress over time and developing a plan for improvement based their individual needs and learning styles.

A comprehensive system of formative assessments, called the NTC Formative Assessment System, is the centerpiece of the NTC mentoring model and training curriculum and is discussed in chapter 3.

PRINCIPLE 4: ENGAGE STAKEHOLDERS AND ALIGN MENTORING WITH INSTRUCTIONAL INITIATIVES

If mentoring programs lack strong partnerships and alignment across the system, they can be undermined. Beginning teachers may receive mixed messages from various support providers and may feel overwhelmed, confused, and frustrated by the various layers of information coming at them. Strong communication and collaboration among stakeholders—including school and district administrators, school board members, union or association leadership, community groups, universities, and professional partners—create a culture of commitment to new teacher support and ensure success across the board.

Effective mentoring programs actively involve these stakeholders in several aspects of the programs, including the recruitment and selection of mentors; the professional development of beginning teachers; site, district, and program orientation; alignment of the mentoring model with local instructional needs; and program evaluation.

Communication and engagement with administrators

Most administrators receive limited, if any, training in their administrative credentialing programs on how to support new teachers. Yet principal support (or its lack) is one of the most influential factors in a new teacher's decision to remain in the classroom.[10]

Strong teacher mentoring programs ensure that site administrators understand the specific needs of new teachers and recognize the importance of the administrative role in setting the stage for the success of beginning teachers and their mentors. Strategic program leaders link mentoring efforts to the many needs, priorities, and goals of site administrators. Moreover, program leaders can articulate how strong, instruction-focused mentoring by carefully selected, highly trained mentors helps achieve a school's goals and supports realization of the principal's vision. Professional development and ongoing communication with principals reinforce their central role in the success of new teachers and provide support for creating conditions that allow new teachers to thrive (e.g., developmentally appropriate class assignments, reduced workload, sufficient resources, professional learning communities, and support from peers).

Historically, most mentoring programs maintain a clear demarcation between teacher mentoring and teacher evaluation. When mentors build confidential relationships with their mentees, the latter can be more open and transparent without fear that exposing their challenges might impact their evaluation. Nonetheless, mentors in effective programs seek to develop strong relationships with principals and take a principal's insights into account when setting mentoring priorities. Mentors can traverse a fine line between confidentiality and disclosure by inviting principal observations and input but withholding their own judgments and evaluation of a teacher's practice.[11]

Partnering with unions and educator associations

Teacher unions and organizations are critical allies in creating high-quality mentoring programs. Their involvement increases program ownership by new and veteran teachers, improves the quality of implementation, reinforces educator professionalism, and heightens respect for teacher leadership—all critical elements of an effective program.

Teacher mentoring represents an opportunity and crossover issue for teacher unions. Although many traditional union ideologies focus on bread-and-butter issues such as salary, benefits, and working conditions, some more progressive associations and unions also are interested in focusing on educational issues that impact student achievement. Because teacher mentoring is closely associated with retention and badly needed support for new teachers, and because high-quality programs ultimately yield stronger student outcomes, unions can become leading advocates for comprehensive mentoring. Programs in districts that contain teacher unions and organizations increase their leverage, and likely improve their outcomes, when deep partnerships are created.

Partnerships with administrator associations are also encouraged. They provide a significant opportunity to learn about the current needs and interests of the principals throughout the system, at the same time capitalizing on the opportunity to communicate with and meet the needs of those principals.

Partnering with universities

Bridging the gap between classroom theory and classroom practice is a persistent challenge, and the teacher mentoring period offers a rich context in which schools and universities can strengthen alignment and support new teachers as they struggle to bridge that gap on a day-to-day basis. Increasingly, universities are becoming involved in their new teachers' lives after graduation and in their first and second years in the classroom.

Many universities are working with local district-led mentoring programs to better align pre-service with mentoring experiences and expectations. Such alignment might include using the same set of professional teaching standards (as a way of providing a common language during the early stages of teacher development) and ensuring that prospective teachers engage in collaborative inquiry from the first moment they enter a credential program through to the mentoring experience.

Having common professional norms across institutions (such as collaborative inquiry, public practice, formative assessment of practice against a set of standards, and the use of assessment of teachers and students to inform teacher practice) offers two benefits. It not only eases the transition from pre-service experience to mentoring but also reinforces behaviors that can support high-quality instruction over a professional lifetime. Mentoring offers a unique and potentially powerful intersection between the two educational contexts—an intersection that can strengthen educator learning and practice in both settings. If what new teachers learn in their pre-service (and alternative certification) programs can be strategically aligned with what they are learning in the classroom, then new teachers will feel more confident and more prepared to address challenges.

Other departments and initiatives

School districts, especially in large urban systems, sometimes tend to develop initiatives in isolation. Competing priorities, turf issues, and historic balkanization inhibit collaboration across programs. These conflicts can create significant obstacles for even the strongest mentoring programs. For example, if a school district (or even a school site) is implementing a specific curriculum and if that initiative is seen as separate from the mentoring program, then new teachers may end up receiving multiple (and possibly competing) layers of support. New teachers often express frustration when programs provide such well-intentioned, but sometimes disconnected, support efforts.

Districts understandably want to provide new teachers with much-needed information on local curricular and instructional initiatives, and schools are eager to get new teachers up and running with regard to site-based professional development efforts. The challenge then becomes how best to align these various efforts to best serve the new teacher. One effective approach is to help the assigned mentor become the broker for the various initiatives. This effort requires that districts identify ways to align the work of the mentors with major curricular and instructional initiatives and then empower mentors to help convey that new knowledge or broker those resources as appropriate to the new teacher's needs and developmental level.

PRINCIPLE 5: COLLECT, ANALYZE, AND COMMUNICATE PROGRAM DATA

Even the most effective mentoring program might not be sustainable if leaders cannot see and understand where the program is working, where improvements can be made, and what the bottom-line outcomes are. Process and outcome data is also essential for program justification and sustainability. Moreover, data helps support quality control of the work of the mentors. Mentors and mentor leaders in high-functioning programs regularly review data to adjust the program, support mentor development, and optimize results.

Formative program data

Just like mentors and teachers, program implementers should collect, analyze, and make decisions based on data. A wide range of data used to inform a cycle of continuous improvement can help programs assess teacher and mentor progress, identify programmatic obstacles, and explore refinements to program design and implementation. Surveys of beginning teachers, mentors, and site administrators can collect triangulated data that provides a broader understanding of the program. Individual mentors can use disaggregated data to help inform their own practice and professional growth, and the aggregated data can inform programmatic decision making. Some data can be shared with site administrators to help them better serve the needs of beginning teachers.

Additional data can be collected following professional development events (beginning teacher seminars and orientations as well as mentor training and meetings) to ensure that each opportunity for learning builds on the last. Constant "dip-sticking" can help programs make ongoing adjustments or provide interventions as needed. More importantly, the ongoing, purposeful collection, analysis, and use of multiple sets of data build congruence across the system. The program is modeling exactly what is being asked of mentors and new teachers—formative assessment. By making this data collection public and by being transparent about how the data influences decision making and program policies, program leaders reinforce the core principle of continuous learning based on rich feedback loops.

Outcome data

Whereas formative data is critical for supporting mentor growth and programmatic decision making, outcome data is critical for understanding a program's impact and for making a strong case for the program's continued existence and support. Data on trends in teacher retention, school movement, student achievement, and other metrics (such as teacher and student absences, student engagement, and so on) can help stakeholders evaluate outcomes. The cost of recruiting and hiring a new teacher makes the retention of successful new teachers, by itself, a desirable program outcome. Often, retention data can most easily be collected.

Finding the data sweet spot involves understanding what the program's context demands vis-à-vis what it can provide. Many large urban districts do not have the infrastructure to collect even teacher retention data, and being able to disaggregate student achievement data by individual teacher offers an insurmountable technical—and, at times, political—obstacle. Program leaders who form a strong relationship with the accountability and data arm of their organization can help collect the available data that can offer insights into a program's impact. Current trends include the improved ability of districts to collect more comprehensive data. The key for programs is to find the data that best relates to significant teacher, student, or organizational (fiscal) outcomes. If funds are available, programs may want to consider occasionally partnering with external providers for the collection of data.

Communication

Stakeholders throughout the system need to know what is happening and whether the substantial investment in mentoring is making a difference. Astute program leaders find ways to articulate their program's value and impact succinctly and strategically—at school board meetings, superintendent cabinets, principal meetings, union leadership councils, and the like. Superintendents and school boards need to know that the money was well spent; principals want to know that students are learning and that the new teachers are adopting the strategies and practices principals want at their schools; teacher and union leaders want to know that their newest members are satisfied and well served.

It's a matter of telling an engaging, meaningful story that speaks to each listener group. Program leaders often find that the most compelling voices are those of the beginning teachers or mentors. Inviting a panel of three or four new teachers to tell the story of their first year and the impact of their mentor on their teaching and their students' learning can resonate far louder than a set of PowerPoint slides. Asking mentors to share how working with new teachers impacted their own understanding of best instruction and their emerging leadership, or asking a new principal who has served as a mentor to describe how observing and mentoring new teachers help make him a more powerful instructional leader—these are the kinds of communication that make the work reverberate.

Each time a program leader disseminates information about the program and its impact, opportunities for increased buy in, collaboration, improvement, and sustainability are likely to emerge. When thoughtfully and strategically conceived, such informational cross-pollination can build political capital and foster a better understanding of instructional mentoring and its potential impact.

PRINCIPLE 6: SUPPORT SCHOOLS TO DEVELOP AN ENVIRONMENT WHERE NEW TEACHERS THRIVE

The principles laid out thus far focus on the development and implementation of mentoring programs. Although mentoring is one key element of an effective induction program, a wide range of policies and practices in the school and district influences the life of a new teacher: how teachers are recruited and hired; how they are placed in an assignment; how courseloads and student placements are determined; whether and how new teachers are oriented to the district, their schools, their colleagues, students, and the broader community; what resources are made available; and how teachers will be evaluated. The list goes on. But beyond even these organizational policies and practices lies a myriad of subtle, powerful cultural practices that contribute to a new teacher's success. Strong induction programs work with schools, teacher associations and unions, and cross-district leadership to consider the broader new teacher experience.

A culture of support for new teachers

In many schools, new teachers get lost in the shuffle that accompanies the start of the school year. Even the most veteran teacher can be overwhelmed by the countless tasks involved in getting ready for the first day of school. Finding time to reach out and fully orient the newest members of the faculty may fall off the plates of well-intentioned administrators or veteran colleagues. New teachers may be starting a new job in a new home in a new community without a supportive social network—something that may not cross the minds of seasoned teachers.

All this newness can be compounded by traditions and cultural practices that make the lives of new teachers harder and not easier. For example, stories abound in which first-year teachers find that their classrooms have been raided for resources (books, chairs, markers, etc.) or that those supplies were allocated the previous spring. Some hypothesize that in the traditional public school culture of scarcity, veteran teachers may consider it an "earned" benefit to have first access to supplies. They may tacitly contribute to the sink-or-swim culture by thinking, "If I went through it, the new kid should have to go through it, too!"

However deeply entrenched such practices might be, mentoring programs can work with principals and other members of the system to support appropriate shifts in culture that foster communities where new teachers will encounter support, fairness, and respect. Research shows that social resources and relationships in schools influence not only student achievement but also the decision of new teachers whether to remain.[12] One solution might be to help schools identify new teacher "buddies," who serve as on-the-spot cultural resources and advocates and whose role and function complement those of the instructional mentor.

Working conditions of beginning teachers

Another way to structure the new teacher's experience for increased success is to address what, in some schools, amounts to a form of new teacher hazing: giving new teachers the most undesirable or most challenging assignments (such as multiple preps at the secondary level, or split or multigraded classrooms at the elementary level), locating their classrooms farthest from administrative or other support, asking them to serve on multiple extra committees, or providing them the least access to the resources they need most to succeed.

In most cases, these well-entrenched traditions and de facto policies have evolved over decades. The solution requires that an entire school embrace the collective responsibility for the success of new colleagues and for the students in new colleagues' classrooms. This approach extends far beyond the purview of most mentoring programs, but program leaders can take on the advocacy role by collecting data, sharing information, raising teacher and administrator awareness, and fostering collaborative outreach across the organization. Reducing teaching loads, providing incentives for veteran teachers to take on the most challenging assignments, considering equitable (and maybe not "equal") allocation of resources, promoting opportunities for the voices of new colleagues to be heard and respected—these policies require a concerted and aligned effort. But the mission that should spur us to action is exactly the same one that demands we seek to level the playing field for diverse student populations: our new teachers deserve similar consideration. Such differentiation extends also to the way in which we provide professional development for new teachers, as discussed next.

Professional development of beginning teachers

Novices are in a unique developmental phase that cannot be addressed by one-size-fits-all workshops or training. When professional development is disconnected from the needs of new teachers, it can feel irrelevant and overwhelming and can lead to increased anxieties and information overload.

Many mentoring programs, in their zeal to provide new teachers with as much information as possible before the start of the school year, can contribute to that overload by offering new teachers multiday, even week-long, new teacher orientations. In effect, these workshops are a pre-service add-on—one more professional development experience before the new teacher actually wraps his arms around his students and curriculum. Current best practices in adult learning point to just-in-time experiences that are linked to students' immediate needs and related to their drive for success. Program leaders may want to consider when and how best to deliver the critical information new teachers need to know. For example, does information about the evaluation process in July or August really stick, or could that be shared at the school sites by the supervising principal or assistant principal? Do new teachers need to know about standardized testing before the school year starts?

Well-qualified and well-trained instructional mentors can deliver, one-on-one—and in the context of the new teacher's classroom—a great deal of curriculum advice and content pedagogy. Mentoring programs may well want to reconsider how much of the content of beginning teacher professional development is appropriate for whole group instruction and how much can be relegated to the interactions between mentors and new teachers. At the same time, professional learning experiences that provide beginning teachers with opportunities to learn outside their specific school context are important; they set the expectation that professional learning takes place both within, and outside, the school site.

Professional learning communities

New teachers can benefit from two types of professional learning communities: one that links them with their rookie peers and a second one that links them with others in similar positions across the spectrum of experience.

Regularly scheduled seminars and online learning communities containing other new teachers provide opportunities for rich networking, professional dialogue, and reflection, as well as help combat isolation. The knowledge that others are experiencing similar challenges and sharing typical new teacher successes are critical support elements. New teacher professional learning communities can address issues that confront all new teachers as well as reinforce norms and practices being fostered by the mentoring component of the program. Such practices include sharing and discussing data concerning classroom practice or student learning; training in professional goal-setting; and reflecting on teaching practices.

Although new teachers need time to connect and learn with other new teachers, they also thrive in environments where they connect and engage in deep learning with colleagues in their school. Well-facilitated grade-level or discipline-focused teams offer opportunities for rigorous conversations about instruction and help new teachers build professional connections with senior staff and build new teachers' knowledge of best practices in teaching and learning. When mentors occasionally are a part of these meetings, they can help new teachers apply the knowledge they have gleaned from these conversations to their classroom practice.

Site-based professional communities of practice help foster collaboration, trust, leadership, and a common vision. It is key that veteran teachers provide an environment that actively engages the new teacher's voice, supports her development, and acknowledges her status as a new (and often extremely enthusiastic and impressionable) learner.

INTERPRETING AND APPLYING THE PRINCIPLES

The principles of high-quality mentoring provide a road map for districts to build or advance programs in ways that have the greatest likelihood of impacting teacher effectiveness and student outcomes. To be successful, such efforts require transforming education policies and structures that may have been in place for many years. They demand that members of the education community push back on the norms that characterized their own individual experiences in schools and rethink and reshape the critical strategies that matter for children: distribution of human resources, rigorous structures for educator learning, data-driven decision making, and infrastructure that builds the human capacity to succeed.

Although these principles provide a platform for engaging in this work of systemic change, the way districts interpret and apply these principles varies greatly across contexts. The nuanced art of implementation leads to what might be perceived as very different programs on the ground, even though they stem from the same intentions and philosophies. The case studies featured in this book provide access to understanding what these principles look like in action at the ground level, focusing on the varying approaches to the work as dictated by each district's history, culture, and ideology.

The one consistent element applied uniformly across all the systems is the work of mentor professional development, including the use of formative assessments and teaching standards. In each of the case studies, NTC is the primary provider of mentor professional development and is responsible for implementing a curriculum of support that has been developed and refined over twenty years. Although the NTC seeks to build the capacity of school district personnel to eventually take over training responsibilities, it often remains the one element that is consistent—and consistently applied—across settings. This particular element of the NTC model is therefore rarely discussed across the case studies. However, the next chapter, chapter 3, is dedicated to articulating the framework of the NTC professional development program, which builds district and school leader knowledge of the complexities of supporting mentors and furthers their ability to implement all aspects of mentoring programs with quality and integrity.

3

Mentor Professional Development

Two decades of experience working with mentor teachers led the New Teacher Center to base its approach to the professional development of mentors on three premises:

- Supporting new teachers is complex and demanding work, and rarely intuitive.

- Exemplary classroom educators do not always become outstanding teacher educators.

- Veteran teachers who step forward to mentor beginning colleagues need time, training, and ongoing support to develop the needed new skills and understanding to be effective.

The result is a rigorous and comprehensive professional development program focused on building the capacity of outstanding educators to become outstanding mentors.[1]

The NTC mentor curriculum is informed by a number of insights, practices, and strategies related to professional learning. They include reflective practice, cognitive coaching, assessment for learning, job-embedded, inquiry-focused learning, brain theory, just-in-time learning, and Jungian operating and learning styles.[2] By building on these best practices, the NTC has created a professional development program that is developmental, responsive, data driven, and recursive.

A FRAMEWORK FOR MENTOR PROFESSIONAL DEVELOPMENT

There is a learning curve associated with any new practice. Just like new teachers, new mentors embark on a process of learning a new job while on the job. Most educators agree that beginning teachers are learning new skills as they develop, but many educators assume that mentoring involves simply transferring a set of skills from the classroom to the adult environment. Being an extraordinary teacher is one of the most important criteria for selecting mentors, but it should never be assumed that mentors know how to mentor simply because they know how to teach.

Work with adult learners has many concepts and practices in common with good classroom teaching, but adult-to-adult professional interactions are sensitive to a number of unique factors. These include age, power, role, judgment, relational trust, school climate, perceptions of competence, and so on. Mentoring takes place in a delicate professional environment over which the mentor has little control, especially when compared with the act of teaching students behind a closed door.

In addition, most experienced teachers have never, themselves, had the opportunity to participate in powerful, dynamic, collaborative partnerships to advance their classroom practice. Although many teachers can bring to mind a trusted colleague who has supported them in their work (often emotionally as well as professionally), very few have had a formal mentoring experience wherein the mentor systematically supports the advancement of the teacher's professional practice. In fact, the traditional concept of "buddy mentor" can be an obstacle to conceptualizing and performing the new role of "instructional mentor." School officials are asking new mentors to create a professional relationship that they are likely never to have experienced and to employ skills and protocols different from those used in the classroom—and to do it in a public, professional context fraught with subtle challenges and potential pitfalls.

Therefore, the NTC's professional development program for mentors views new mentors as emerging practitioners who develop their craft over time as they accrue training, inquiry, and experience. This developmental approach to mentor learning means that up-front professional development is only the first step. Just as beginning teachers benefit from ongoing support and learning, so do mentors. Many programs mandate a series of training sessions for mentors early in or prior to the start of the school year and then presume that this initial training fully equips mentors to take on the work. Although foundational training is essential, it should not constitute the only, or even the bulk of, mentor learning. If mentors are to develop into highly skilled teacher educators who can serve as vanguard change agents, then their professional development needs to be chunked, carefully sequenced, and delivered over time. Like their new teachers, mentors need just-in-time learning that systematically develops their skills.

NTC mentor curriculum

The NTC's curriculum for mentor development has emerged over many years (and is continually being refined) as program leaders, mentors, and professional developers continually seek to answer the critical question: What do instructional mentors need to know and do to accelerate new teacher practice, improve student learning, and foster professional norms of inquiry and continual professional improvement? This chapter seeks to answer that question and provide glimpses into the tools, strategies, and approaches developed to build mentor capacity in the areas described.

Note that several threads are woven throughout the NTC's professional development program. They are not treated as separate curricular topics addressed only at a specific stage in the mentor's development. Instead, they are made explicit and are revisited recursively throughout the curriculum. They include the following:

- *Mentoring for what?* The purpose of instructional mentoring is to accelerate the development of every new teacher. Given that low-income and urban students of color in the United States are significantly more likely to be taught by new teachers than experienced ones, mentors have an added obligation to help ensure that these new colleagues will be able to teach these children effectively.

- *Issues of equity:* Mentors must be advocates for the academic success of each student. This requires that instructional mentors learn to help a new teacher recognize and address—with poise, confidence, and persistence—issues related to race, language, and culture as they play out in the educational environment.

- *Change agentry:* Mentors cannot simply be purveyors of the status quo. The mentor's role can and should be transformational, and this requires that the mentor be both responsive to and responsible for helping change the system as needed.

- *Mentors as learners:* The mentor role is a new leadership role for teachers, and it requires a learning stance. The charge of developing teachers for the next generation of students requires new strategies, new techniques, and new knowledge.

Woven together, these threads underlie a mentoring curriculum that builds upon the knowledge and understanding of excellent teachers. But rather than focus on the learning needs of classroom students, mentors are trained to strategically respond to the professional needs of new colleagues. The purpose is the same: to advance the learning and achievement of others. The following pages highlight some of the key components of this curriculum and a number of insights into mentor learning.

A TRUSTING RELATIONSHIP

The NTC believes that a mentor's success depends on the mentor's ability to quickly forge a strong, trusting relationship with a new colleague. If a new teacher does not trust the mentor, she will not be receptive to the support the mentor provides, and the impact on her practice will be limited.

Mentor training explicitly addresses issues of trust and teaches specific strategies that support strong, trusting professional relationships. These methods include the use of nonjudgmental language, a belief in the autonomy of the new teacher, support for the new teacher's own decision making, the ability to tailor support to the needs of the new teacher, and mentor behaviors such as reliability, honesty, and sincerity.[3]

In the early stages of the relationship, mentors are encouraged to ensure that they are responsive, value-added problem solvers who do not impose their agenda over that of the new teacher's. Trust can be further cemented when mentors quickly enter into a collaborative partnership focused on gathering and understanding data about student learning and addressing those needs, rather than critiquing the new teacher's performance.

THE INSTRUCTIONAL MENTOR'S ROLE

Great mentoring should convey the complexity of teaching and engage new teachers in the professional norms of collaborative inquiry, formative assessment informed by data, and ongoing learning. Helping mentors frame and understand their multifaceted role as mentors and their responsibility for helping shape the next generation of educators is an explicit component of the NTC mentoring curriculum. Central to this role is the understanding that an instructional mentor's explicit charge is to advance the new teacher's classroom effectiveness on behalf of students—an outcome that extends far beyond friendly, collegial support. An instructional mentor's key responsibility is to improve student learning in each new teacher's classroom.

Mentoring is approached by the NTC as an opportunity for learning as much as for teaching. Mentors are encouraged to become inquirers into their own mentoring practice, to use data, and to model curiosity and ongoing learning. The curriculum encourages them to use language of tentativeness and flexibility, multiple options and persistence. The intent is for mentors to convey that effective teaching is not simply a matter of having the one right instructional strategy that will work under all circumstances. Experience shows that there are no pat answers to complex issues of learning and teaching, and narrow, prescriptive approaches to children and their individual development are not likely to be the most effective.

NTC's mentor professional development program involves more than talk about the desired behaviors and practices. Instead, veteran educators step into this new leadership role to experience and practice some of the norms that may not be part of the existing school culture. Mentors are encouraged to see themselves as transformational change agents who have the power to inculcate, one teacher at a time, practices and attitudes that will last these newcomers a professional lifetime.

MENTORING APPROACHES

If they don't know how to communicate their expertise in ways that make new teachers want to listen, even the most talented veteran teachers—those who have extraordinary knowledge and skills—may not make good mentors. Without training, new mentors often employ a "tell-them-what-I-know" approach. This method feels good for the mentor wanting to impart wisdom, but it usually fails to build a new teacher's capacity to succeed.

This is similar to the "friendly advice ignored" paradigm. Consider a person—let's call her Teresa—who goes to a friend—Michelle—with a problem. In an effort to support Teresa, Michelle gives thoughtful, sound, and viable advice. Teresa is thrilled to hear the wonderful news that there is hope for resolution of the issue, but days later Michelle learns that Teresa has ignored the advice and gotten deeper into the problem. It is not that the advice was bad but rather that Teresa has little ownership of it. It was not her idea. Or she doesn't understand how to implement the advice. Or she is afraid that she does not have the skills to implement the advice effectively.

With this in mind, the NTC curriculum focuses on helping mentors develop the language, approaches, and strategies necessary to get them out of advice-giver mode and into the role of knowledgeable guide and strategic facilitator of teacher learning as well as persistent advocate for student achievement. NTC professional development takes mentors through several layers of understanding, including the following.

Mentoring language

Drawing from the knowledge base of coaching, mentors learn to use the techniques of active listening, paraphrasing, clarifying, and reflective questioning. These language skills ensure that mentors carefully listen to, understand, and focus on what new teachers are saying (or not saying) rather than on what the mentor knows and wants to impart. Careful questioning helps extend new teachers' thinking and supports their problem-solving skills and personal agency.

Questions also help convey the complexity of teaching and the need for ongoing inquiry into practice. Mentors learn to offer suggestions in ways that build new teacher ownership of the solution or possible next steps. This approach helps engender a sense that the mentor is truly interested in learning about the new teacher's needs and is 100 percent focused on his individual professional success. By using language that invites teachers to consider evidence of student learning, mentors help new teachers base their decision-making on student needs.

Instructive, collaborative, facilitative (ICF)

The NTC curriculum includes a range of mentoring approaches that are conveyed using what it calls the instructive, collaborative, facilitative (ICF) framework.[4] Mentors learn how and when to be *instructive* (providing insights, suggestions, and ideas based on their own knowledge), *collaborative* (working with the new teacher to brainstorm new strategies and collaboratively solve problems), or *facilitative* (asking guiding questions that permit the new teacher to reflect, make connections, and drive her own learning).

Introduced early in the mentor curriculum, ICF is revisited throughout the course of mentor learning. Mentors develop skills in using the approaches seamlessly as they respond to cues from new teachers, much as a skillful dancer responds to a partner's subtle movements and the rhythm of the music. When used artfully, ICF helps a mentor guide a new teachers' decision making while building professional confidence and autonomy.

Entry points

A subtle mentoring skill is the ability to identify and strategically use *entry points* for learning. Because mentors are trained to allow new teachers to determine focus areas and drive the learning, mentors must become adept at providing small, powerful, just-in-time chunks of knowledge.

For example, a new teacher remarks, "Oh, Jake just doesn't get math. The other third-grade teachers say neither of his brothers did well in math, so he doesn't have a chance." This incident offers a mentor an entry point to support the new teacher in examining expectations and discovering ways to support Jake's learning. Using the facilitative approach, the mentor might ask guiding questions about whether there are times when Jake seems to "get math" and what sorts of learning tasks seem to be easier for him; probing more deeply, the mentor might invite the teacher to reflect on how her expectations might impact Jake's behavior. Depending on the teacher's response, the mentor might also use an instructive approach to talk about research that shows the importance of teacher perceptions and expectations to student performance. Or using the collaborative approach, the mentor might brainstorm with the new teacher ways to address Jake's learning needs.

Mentors also learn to use student assessment data and student work as powerful entry points for teacher development. By focusing on the students, a mentor can enter into a collaborative partnership with the new teacher that concentrates on helping students reach important learning outcomes. In this case, the mentor might review several completed Analyzing Student Work protocols (described later in this chapter) to identify areas where Jake was meeting or exceeding expectations in math throughout the year. This can support the teacher's self-realization that Jake can achieve at high levels in some skills and that blanket or negative expectations are not reflective of students' actual abilities or potential. The data on student learning thus becomes an independent arbiter of teacher effectiveness and helps instill a student-centered approach to instruction that can subvert negative (or unrealistic) expectations.

Needs of beginning teachers

As the National Commission on Teaching and America's Future states in its 2003 report, *No Dream Denied*, "Teachers are not 'finished products' when they complete a teacher preparation program." Regardless of the quality or duration of the teacher preparation program, new teachers assume the full range of teacher responsibilities only on the first day on the job. Everything before that might be considered a simulation. Pre-service cannot substitute for the unique experiences of the first two or three years of practice.

It's a complex process to apply theory learned in pre-service education (or alternative certification programs) to the day-to-day reality of classroom teaching. New teachers find themselves juggling the demands of new curricula, programs, resources, testing protocols, and mandates while simultaneously trying to access and apply what they learned in pre-service. This is a unique phase of development, and the NTC mentor curriculum helps mentors develop an understanding of the challenges associated with being a new teacher who is often asked to assume the same responsibilities as the most veteran teachers in the system.

Mentors are supported in developing an understanding of the attitudinal phases of new teacher development as well as the need to capitalize on new teachers' existing knowledge and experiences.[5] Mentors are encouraged to help make their own thinking and problem solving accessible to new teachers to help them connect theory and practice and to convey the complexity of teaching—all this while supporting the passion, commitment, and desire for success that most new teachers bring to the profession.

Adult learning

Understanding the needs of adult learners is another important component of the mentor's curriculum. Adults learn while on the job and therefore are likely to be much more engaged learners when the new ideas or strategies are directly linked to their professional success.

Given the many competing demands of any complex professional environment, adults tend to seek out just-in-time learning that focuses on their immediate needs. Mentors are trained to capitalize on these developmental entry points and bring their knowledge and insights to the table just when the new teacher is most likely to be able to hear, understand, and use the information. Mentors are also supported in learning how to help new teachers build on their classroom successes rather than focus only on their challenges and struggles, even though most new teachers obsessively focus on what's wrong in the classroom.

New teachers come to teaching with a set of personal experiences on which the mentor can build; in fact, one might argue that teaching is unique among professions in that the novice comes to the practice with more than seventeen years of experience (as a student), albeit as a consumer and observer. When mentors recognize and draw links to the adult learner's prior knowledge, they not only more effectively engage the new teacher but also build an increased sense of ownership and professional competence.

Understanding and articulating effective instruction

If the instructional mentor's primary goal is to advance new teachers' classroom practice toward high-quality instruction, then mentors need to recognize and understand the commonly identified elements of high-quality instruction. Often, it is assumed that outstanding teachers automatically have this knowledge; yet many talented educators may not know what it is about their teaching that is so effective.[6] Few teachers are called upon to articulate what makes their teaching effective, and few have observed and analyzed a colleague's practice.

The teaching profession's historic lack of a common language to describe effective instruction contributes to this dilemma. If you ask a dozen educators what effective instruction looks like, you will often get a dozen different answers. Although talented educators may cite specific strategies they find effective (differentiated instruction, higher-order thinking skills, assessment of learning, cooperative learning, etc.), few can articulate the specific underlying knowledge and skills that make these strategies effective. Thus, one of the most important components of the NTC mentor curriculum is to help mentors become familiar with the language of best practice.

Like mentoring programs across California, the NTC turns to the California Standards for the Teaching Profession (CSTP), which were adopted by the California Board of Education and the Commission on Teacher Credentialing more than ten years ago. The standards enable mentors, administrators, and teachers to speak a common language about instruction no matter which pathway, training, and preparation program brought them to their particular school context.

Organized into six overarching categories, the structure of the CSTP also contributes to its usefulness. Within each standard is a set of *key elements,* which further articulates effective practices. These key elements are explained, not by a checkoff list of behaviors and skills, but by a series of five to ten *indicator questions,* which invite mentors and beginning teachers to consider what those practices look like and the extent to which they are being implemented in the classroom.[7] A page from the CSTP (see figure 3-1) illustrates the unique format and accessibility of the standards.

In other states, the NTC works with the National Board for Professional Teaching Standards (NBPTS) Core Propositions, Charlotte Danielson's Four Domains, and sets of professional standards developed by state agencies across the country. Some districts and organizations have worked with the NTC to design their standards in a format similar to the CSTP and describe specifics of best practice through reflective questions. The NTC mentor curriculum teaches these various sets of professional standards to build mentors' skills in articulating and identifying best practices.

Incremental development of new teachers

Although professional teaching standards provide the common language, elements, and reflective questions that frame high-quality instruction, they

FIGURE 3-1 Sample page from the California Standards for the Teaching Profession

Engaging Students in Learning

Connecting students' prior knowledge, life experience, and interests with learning goals.

As teachers develop, they may ask, "How do I..." or "Why do I..."

- help students to see the connections between what they already know and the subject matter?
- help students connect classroom learning to their life experiences and cultural understanding?
- support all students to use first and second language skills to achieve learning goals?
- open a lesson or unit to capture student attention and interest?
- build on students' comments and questions during a lesson to extend their understanding?
- make "on the spot" changes in my teaching based on students' interests and questions?

Promoting self-directed, reflective learning for all students.

As teachers develop, they may ask, "How do I..." or "Why do I..."

- motivate students to initiate their own learning and to strive for challenging learning goals?
- encourage all students to describe their own learning processes and progress?
- explain clear learning goals for all students of each activity or lesson?
- engage all students in opportunities to examine and evaluate their own work and to learn from the work of their peers?
- help all students to develop and use strategies for knowing about, reflecting on, and monitoring their own learning?
- help all students to develop and use strategies for accessing knowledge and information?

Using a variety of instructional strategies and resources to respond to students' diverse needs

As teachers develop, they may ask, "How do I..." or "Why do I..."

- engage students in a variety of learning experiences to address the different ways they learn?
- use a variety of strategies to introduce, explain, and restate subject matter concepts and processes so that ALL students understand?
- choose strategies that make the complexity and depth of subject matter understandable to all students, including second language learners?
- vary my instructional strategies to increase students' active participation in learning?
- ask questions or facilitate discussion to clarify or extend students' thinking?
- make use of unexpected events to augment student learning?
- recognize when a lesson is falling apart and what do I do about it?

Facilitating learning experiences that promote autonomy, interaction, and choice.

As teachers develop, they may ask, "How do I..." or "Why do I..."

- use the classroom environment to provide opportunities for independent and collaborative learning?
- participate in and promote positive interactions between all students?
- support and monitor student autonomy and choice during learning experiences?
- support and monitor student collaboration during learning activities?
- help students make decisions about managing time and materials during learning activities?

Standard for Engaging and Supporting All Students in Learning

Teachers build on students' prior knowledge, life experience, and interests to achieve learning goals for all students. Teachers use a variety of instructional strategies and resources that respond to students' diverse needs. Teachers facilitate challenging learning experiences for all students in environments that promote autonomy, interaction, and choice. Teachers actively engage all students in problem solving and critical thinking within and across subject matter areas. Concepts and skills are taught in ways that encourage students to apply them in real-life contexts that make subject matter meaningful. Teachers assist all students to become self-directed learners who are able to demonstrate, articulate, and evaluate what they learn.

Source: California Department of Education. California Commission on Teacher Credentialing. California Standards for the Teaching Profession, 1997, http://www.ctc.ca.gov/reports/cstpreport.pdf.

do not articulate what developing practice looks like in the classroom at various levels. For mentors and new teachers to frame their work together, they need to assess the extent to which the new teachers are moving toward the high levels of practice described by the standards in ways that help new teachers and mentors focus their next steps of support and growth.

As early as 1991, the Santa Cruz New Teacher Project collaborated with the California Department of Education to craft an outline of a developmental continuum, with beginning and advanced levels of classroom practice. The NTC's Continuum of Teacher Development, fully aligned with the CSTP, is the evolved version of that work. The intent is not only to describe the incremental stages of a teacher's developing practice in each of the standard areas but also to convey that a teacher's development continues over a professional career.

The Continuum also suggests that the expectations we set for all teachers should be commensurate with their experience, skills, dispositions, and areas of expertise.

A sample page of the Continuum is shown in figure 3-2. This sample page is one of two provided for the standard titled Engaging and Supporting All Students in Learning.

The column labeled "Beginning" highlights what one might expect practice to look like for a new teacher who has completed a teacher preparation program. To avoid suggesting that beginning stages of practice are deficits rather than developmentally appropriate levels of proficiency, the Continuum uses positive language even at the beginning level. It assumes that every teacher has some knowledge and skills in effective instruction, even if they are in a nascent stage. This assumption allows mentors and new teachers to focus on what is working rather than on areas where they are less effective (a common tendency of new teachers that perpetuates a lack of confidence and low morale).

"Emerging" describes a level of teacher practices that one might expect for teachers who have developed beyond the beginning stages—something that might be expected of a teacher after a few months of practice. The remaining columns ("Applying," "Integrating," and "Innovating") lay out the developmental progression of a teacher's practice to the highest levels of classroom instruction and provide a road map for development over a career.

FIGURE 3-2 Sample page from the New Teacher Center's Continuum of Teacher Development

Engaging and Supporting All Students in Learning

	Beginning	Emerging	Applying	Integrating	Innovating
Connecting students' prior knowledge, life experience, and interests with learning goals	Opens lesson to capture students' attention and interest. Teacher recognizes the value of students' prior knowledge and life experiences.	Asks questions that elicit students' prior knowledge, life experiences and interests. Some connections are made to the learning goals and objectives of the lesson.	Implements activities and elicits questions that help students make connections between what they already know and the learning goals and objectives.	Uses questions and activities to extend students' abilities to integrate what they know with the learning goals and objectives. Makes adjustments during lesson to ensure that all students meet the learning goals.	Creates a context for students to synthesize learning goals and objectives with what they know and develop their own complementary learning goals.
Using a variety of instructional strategies and resources to respond to students' diverse needs	Uses a few instructional strategies. Delivers instruction with available resources and materials.	Varies instruction to increase student participation. Selects strategies, resources, and visuals with some consideration of students' academic and linguistic needs.	Elicits student participation through a variety of instructional strategies intended to match students' academic and linguistic needs. Checks for student understanding.	Uses a repertoire of strategies and resources. Selects and differentiates learning to accommodate students' diverse learning styles.	Uses extensive repertoire of strategies to meet students' diverse academic and linguistic needs and ensure fullest participation and learning for all students.
Facilitating learning experiences that promote autonomy, interaction, and choice	Directs learning experiences through whole group and individual work with possibilities for interaction and choice.	Varies learning experiences to include work in large groups and small groups, with student choice within learning activities.	Provides learning experiences utilizing individual and group structures to develop autonomy and group participation skills. Students make choices about and within their work.	Uses a variety of learning experiences to assist students in developing independent working skills and group participation skills. Supports students in making appropriate choices for learning.	Integrates a variety of challenging learning experiences that develop students' independent learning, collaboration, and choice.

Source: © 2004 New Teacher Center at the University of California, Santa Cruz.

The document conveys NTC's underlying philosophy that learning to teach well is a lifelong endeavor. Even the most accomplished veteran teachers will find areas for continued growth and development.

Mentors learn to use the Continuum of Teacher Development collaboratively with their beginning teachers to identify specific goals, assess progress, and determine entry points for improving practice. New teachers come to realize that they are embarking on a pathway to excellence and that it's OK to be a beginner. As novices assess their own work, mentors encourage them to cite evidence and examples to support the assessment.

Mentors also encourage new teachers to focus on a subset of elements. Because the six CSTP standards contain intentional redundancies and links, the NTC believes that advancing the teacher's practice in one standard area will simultaneously advance it in others. Taking on all six standards and all thirty-six elements of effective teaching is an overwhelming, overly ambitious approach that leads to little depth of development in any particular area.

Just as new teachers are taught to analyze student work to better design instruction, mentors learn to use the Continuum to help analyze evidence of a new teacher's developing practice and tailor support to be most strategic. NTC is also working with a number of districts to incorporate the use of the Continuum into the local teacher tenure or evaluation system, particularly as a tool for professional goal-setting. In any case, the NTC stresses the importance of developing realistic, yet rigorous, expectations for new teachers.

Tools and protocols to support dialogue and formative assessment

The key to effective instructional mentoring is systematic, focused support for the acceleration of a new teacher's instructional practice. The power of the mentoring may be compromised when interactions are informal, unfocused, or unrelated to instruction and student learning. If interactions between mentors and beginning teachers lack a structure and focus on classroom practice (supported by data gathered through classroom observations, teacher reflection and assessment, and student work), then interactions may become, by default, more traditional "buddy" mentoring.

Many mentors face two challenges as they step into this role. First, most school cultures do not prepare mentors to engage in and support the thoughtful identification, analysis, and collaborative problem solving of issues in instructional practice.[8] The norms of open and honest communication, public sharing of instructional dilemmas (and successes), and sanctioned opportunities to reflect on practice are not yet part of the professional lives of most teachers. In fact, many educators have been conditioned to avoid this kind of professional learning. Second, mentors do not come into the field of mentoring knowing how to collect data about a teacher's practice. We have, indeed, encountered twenty- and twenty-five-year veteran teachers who become mentors without ever having had the opportunity to watch a colleague teach.

To support mentors as they engage in professional dialogue supported by data regarding practice, the NTC has developed a set of protocols and tools that helps mentors overcome these barriers to collaborative work while helping new teachers create systematic documentation of their growth and development.

The NTC Formative Assessment System (FAS) helps guide the mentor's interactions with new teachers and supports the collection of data on multiple aspects of a teacher's practice to be used as a guide for informing instructional growth. FAS includes an array of seventeen protocols and supporting tools (with additional tools in development). Mentors are trained to identify cues and entry points in the teacher's practice that suggest the use of a FAS tool to serve as a strategic lever for prompting and guiding a conversation that supports new teacher growth. It is not the tool itself, but the critical dialogue it structures, that allows new teachers to have "aha!" moments and develop the habits of mind that lead to more-effective teaching.

Mentors and district leaders are cautioned not to let these tools become forms to be filled out rather than platforms for grappling with critical elements of instruction. Each tool is carefully designed to serve both the mentor and the new teacher. For the mentor, it is a convenient structure for professional dialogue that leads to greater clarity about the new teacher's developmental needs; for the new teacher, it helps document growth and progress while conveying essential approaches to effective instruction.[9]

The use of protocols and tools, however, is not a common practice, and so the NTC mentor curriculum includes intensive training on how to use the tools skillfully and to greatest effect. When used well—when the data collected is shared in ways that help new teachers develop the skills to reflect on, analyze, and drive their own learning—these tools help mentor and teacher move to the heart of teacher effectiveness: what are my students learning? How well? And what can I do, as a teacher, to improve that learning? Mentors stop telling teachers what to do and instead facilitate a process whereby new teachers figure out how to accelerate their own practice. This result yields a cadre of teachers (along with their mentors) who are motivated and able to engage in ongoing inquiry using data to improve their instructional practice well after the mentoring program is over.

Next, we look at three of the seventeen FAS tools and describe how to use them effectively.

Collaborative Assessment Log. The Collaborative Assessment Log (CAL) is the fundamental FAS tool (see figure 3-3). Typically used every time a mentor and new teacher meet, the CAL is used not only to collect data on the new teacher's development but also to guide the mentoring conversation. It has three basic purposes: it provides a context for the work to help focus the conversation on instruction; it helps new teachers focus on and build on what's working, in addition to assessing challenges; and it guides mentor and beginning teachers in articulating specific next steps and thus become accountable to one another.

The six professional teaching standards are listed at the bottom of the log, and mentors are trained to incorporate the standards into the conversations as they identify the strengths and challenges in the teacher's practice. By ensuring a focus on the standards, the log helps mentors and new teachers talk about the specific elements of instruction that matter most in the moment. This focus reduces the time spent in unfocused conversations (which may be important in small doses but will not lead to changed practice if that becomes the bulk of the conversation).

Guided by the notion that the advancement of practice builds upon successes, the first quadrant in the CAL invites new teachers to identify what is working in their classrooms. This is a very different approach from the one many new teachers take; they tend to focus on what isn't working in their classrooms. Overwhelmed by day-to-day challenges and glitches and having set impossibly high bars for themselves, new teachers often fail to recognize the things that are going well.

FIGURE 3-3 A sample Collaborative Assessment Log

Collaborative Assessment Log

Name: _Kira_   Mentor: _Alicia_

Grade Level/Subject Area: _K, 1st, 2nd   Multi-Graded_   Date: _9/11_

class support

Check all that apply:
- ○ Analyzing Student Work
- ✗ Communicating with Parents
- ○ Discussing Content Standards
- ○ Developing/Reviewing Professional Goals
- ○ Discussing Case Study Student
- ○ IEP Development/Meeting
- ○ Modeling Lesson
- ○ Observing Instruction
- ○ Observing Veteran Teacher
- ○ Planning Lesson
- ✗ Problem Solving
- ○ Providing Resources
- ○ Pre-Observation Conference
- ○ Post-Observation Conference
- ✗ Reflecting
- ○ Using Technology
- ○ Other

What's Working:

- Students beginning to use systems/procedures, especially for transitions.
- Two parents volunteering in class
- Read alouds have been very successful

Current Focus—Challenges—Concerns:

- Not sure how to use help of parents without "losing control" of class
- Multi-graded (K, 1, 2) planning is challenging
- Wide range of abilities and needs.

Teacher's Next Steps:

- assess students
- Develop a plan for parent participation and support
  - Get 2 clip boards
  - Write up goals/task/feedback tool

Mentor's Next Steps:

- Support assessments with initial modeling of district assessments (Dibels)
- Teach math lesson—while Kira assesses students—one to one
- Share Tomlinson How to Differentiate Instr. in Mixed—Ability Classrooms (Flow Chart)

Next Meeting Date: 9/18		Focus: Modeling Lesson

EN=Engaging and Supporting All Students in Learning	EE=Creating & Maintaining an Effective Environment	SM=Understanding and Organizing Subject Matter	PL=Planning Instruction and Designing Learning Experiences	AS=Assessing Student Learning	DP=Developing as a Professional Educator
• Connecting students' prior knowledge, life experience, and interests with learning goals	• Creating a physical environment that engages all students	• Demonstrating knowledge of subject matter content and student development	• Drawing on and valuing students' backgrounds, interests, and developmental learning needs	• Establishing and communicating learning goals for all students	• Reflecting on teaching practices and planning professional development
• Using a variety of instructional strategies and resources to respond to students' diverse needs	• Establishing a climate that promotes fairness and respect	• Organizing curriculum to support student understanding of subject matter	◉ Establishing and articulating goals for student learning	◉ Collecting and using multiple sources of information to assess student learning	• Establishing professional goals and pursuing opportunities to grow professionally
• Facilitating learning experiences that promote autonomy, interaction, and choice	• Promoting social development and group responsibility	• Interrelating ideas and information within and across subject matter areas	• Developing and sequencing instructional activities and materials for student learning	• Involving and guiding all students in assessing their own learning	• Working with communities to improve professional practice
• Engaging students in problem solving, critical thinking, and other activities that make subject matter meaningful	◉ Establishing and maintaining standards for student behavior _(parent groups)_	• Developing student understanding through instructional strategies that are appropriate to the subject matter	• Designing short-term and long-term plans to foster student learning	◉ Using the results of assessment to guide instruction	◉ Working with families to improve _parent volunteer_ professional practice
• Promoting self-directed, reflective learning for all students	✱ • Planning and implementing classroom procedures and routines that support student learning	• Using materials, resources and technologies to make subject matter accessible to students	• Modifying instructional plans to adjust for student needs → _as a result_	• Communicating with students, families, and other audiences about student progress	• Working with colleagues to improve professional practice
	• Using instructional time effectively				• Balancing professional responsibilities and maintaining motivation

Source: © 2004 New Teacher Center at the University of California, Santa Cruz.

Mentors use their language skills to elicit successes and challenges and to probe for specificity as the new teachers reflect on and assess their experiences since the last conversation. Helping new teachers reflect on what's working allows them to build on the elements of their practice that are effective while building their confidence that they are becoming effective practitioners. Articulating successes can also encourage them to be more open about the challenges in their practice.

After gathering data about successes and challenges and using the new teacher's own language cues as an entry point, the mentor helps focus the assessment on an area of challenge that is likely to best support the teacher's developing effectiveness. Using a range of approaches (instructive, collaborative, and facilitative, as discussed earlier in this chapter), the mentor works with the new teacher to identify developmentally appropriate strategies and ideas. The CAL helps ensure that the mentoring is tailored to the assessed skills, knowledge, and interests of the new teacher, further supporting the novice's developing autonomy.

A critical element of this conversation is to identify and list specific next steps for both parties. This section of the CAL supports the teacher in taking action and applying new learning to his regular practice; and because mentors follow up on the next steps in the next meeting, new teachers are gently held accountable for taking action. With next steps clearly documented, mentors, too, are held accountable for the resources and support they agreed to provide. In addition, the next-steps section assists the mentor in following up and preparing for the next meeting so that the new teacher's progress can be systematically accelerated.

Another positive consequence of the CAL is that it tracks progress over time. When mentors use the CAL each time they meet with their beginning teachers, they create a record that captures instructional growth. For example, if a new teacher is working primarily on classroom management strategies at the beginning of the year and by February is using differentiated instruction to support student engagement, the CAL helps the teacher reflect on her practice and say, "It was just after winter break when I realized that trying new instructional strategies to meet the different learning styles in my room actually drastically improved my classroom management issues."

A final benefit of the CAL is that mentors can use it to benchmark the successes they are having with their assigned teachers and to develop a better sense of when and how approaches to mentoring will be best received. For example, if the mentor notices that most of the teachers are starting to understand in February why assessments of students are important for lesson planning, then the mentor can consider how to create entry points in January that help all his teachers to that realization.

Selective Scripting. The Selective Scripting tool is based on well-established practices of coaching designed to capture a teacher's exact language and specific behaviors as well as those of the students.[10] By seeing a verbatim scripting of their language and their accompanying behaviors (as well as those of their students), new teachers can step back and gain a perspective on their practice they wouldn't otherwise have gained (see figure 3-4). Few teachers get to hear what they sound like when they are speaking, and sometimes they don't understand why students react the way they do. The Selective Scripting tool gives them a more objective understanding of their instructional delivery and lets them make observations that can lead to improved practice in the very next lesson.

The tool is called Selective Scripting for two reasons. First, it is not expected that the mentor will capture everything the new teacher is saying or doing—a technique that often discourages mentors and overwhelms teachers. Instead, mentors are trained to collect *sentence stems*—strategic parts of sentences and phrases used during instructional delivery—when observing a teacher in action. Second, the observation data is restricted to a particular instructional or behavioral focus that the mentor and new teacher have identified collaboratively before the observation and, whenever possible, have linked to the new teacher's professional goals. The focus is noted at the top of the page and guides both the mentor's collection and the collaborative analysis of the data. The same selectivity applies to the data about what the students are saying and doing in response to the teacher's instruction.

The mentor also records the elapsed time in the left column. The goal is to have sufficient data to help the new teacher better understand his practice and provide an entry point for the mentor to assist the teacher's

FIGURE 3-4 A sample Selective Scripting tool

FORMATIVE ASSESSMENT TOOL

Selective Scripting

Name: _Margie_   Mentor: _Maria_

Grade Level/Subject Area: _Third_   Date: _11/12_

Lesson Topic: _Writing, correct use of past +_   Teaching Standard: _Engaging Students, Subject Matter_
present tenses
Observation Focus: _Participation, Engagement_   Content Standard: _1.0, 1.8, Writing_

Time	Teacher	Students
12:50	If you're ready, thumbs up.	7 students put thumbs up
	_____ is ready _____ is ready	6 more put thumbs up
	We're going to look at words ending in /ed/ and /d/ today.	
	When do words have /ed/ or /d/ as their ending?	▲▲▲ They already happened. (Cody) It was in the past. (Melissa)
	Yes, /d/ & /ed/ tell us the action happened in the past.	
	Teacher passes out text to each student. Students get different reading levels of text "Please read your paragraph and highlight all the /d & /ed/ words"	All students participating and highlighting (very quiet) working indep. and silently
	Monitored, walked around, checked in with 6 students	Teacher like this?
	No, just circle the /ed/ and /d/ endings	
	Continued check-in, support as needed	
	Helped Chelsea find a few that she missed. "Read this sentence to me..."	Chelsea reads the sentence, finds another /ed/ word
12:55	Vicente—Since you are done, will you start collecting highlighters	Vicente picks up highlighters

Code: ▲ hand raised

Source: © 2004 New Teacher Center at the University of California, Santa Cruz.

FIGURE 3-4 (*continued*)

Selective Scripting

Name: _Margie_   Mentor: _Maria_

Grade Level/Subject Area: _____   Date: _11/12_

Lesson Topic: _____   Teaching Standard: _____

Observation Focus: _____   Content Standard: _____

Time	Teacher	Students
12:58	Let's make a list of our /ed/ & /d/ words Teacher records words under 2 columns—/ed/d /ed/ /d/ walked created jumped shared needed used picked taped	Students share words—students selected at random—teacher pulled names from jar
1:07	OK. Let's look at the words in these 2 columns. What do all the words in the /d/ column have in common? Teacher underlines root words 5 seconds wait time before anyone raises hand. Teresa Yes—they do. Thank you. Now, what do all the words in the /ed/ column have in common? Kevin? Yes. Does anyone remember what letters that aren't vowels are called?	♠♠ They all end in /e/ (Teresa) ♠♠♠♠♠ They don't end in /e/ (Kevin)
1:13	/e/ is an example of a vowel. /k/ is an example of a consonant. All the words in the /ed/ column end in consonants. So, past tense words end in /ed/ when the word ends w/a consonant and /d/ when it ends in /e/. Any questions?	No student response

Code: ♠ hand raised

Source: © 2004 New Teacher Center at the University of California, Santa Cruz.

advancement. Mentors usually find that a ten-minute set of selective data is more than adequate to prompt a rich post-observation discussion.

After the observation, mentors lead the new teacher through an examination of the data, inviting him to note particular exchanges with students, patterns of behavior (student or teacher), surprises, or positive examples of his developing practice. The mentors guide teachers to make connections between what they are doing and saying and how, and whether, students are learning.

Analysis of Student Work. It's critical for teachers to assess student learning in ways that identify students' learning needs and then use that knowledge to design effective instruction. This process requires a complex set of sophisticated skills. Given, however, that this ability goes to the heart of understanding learning needs and helping all students achieve, mentors are trained to support new teachers in the analysis of student work to inform instruction.

The Analysis of Student Work (ASW) tool (shown in figure 3-5) gives mentors a protocol to help new teachers think through the steps of determining whether students are learning, where particular students' strengths and gaps may be, and, most importantly, how to tailor instruction to meet the needs of the students. What makes the FAS Analysis of Student Work protocol unusual is that it explicitly draws links between the analysis and the teacher's instructional next steps.

Mentors ask new teachers ahead of time to assign and collect samples of student work (an essay, a math work sheet, results from a recent assessment, etc.). The mentors then guide the new teachers through a four-stage protocol that helps build the habits of mind that help teachers address each student's learning needs. Professional development supports mentors in thoroughly understanding the tool as well as becoming familiar with mentoring language that can help deepen the new teacher's examination, analysis, and differentiation.

Mentors begin by asking new teachers to think about and articulate what they expected from their students on the given assignment. This helps the new teacher understand how critical it is that she set and articulate her expectations and the standards of success before each task or

FIGURE 3-5 A sample Analysis of Student Work tool

Analysis of Student Work

Name: _Margie_   Mentor: _Maria_

Grade Level/Subject Area: _Third_   Date: _10/25_

Student Work Selected for Analysis: _Writing–Paragraph_   Content Standard: 1.0 Capitalization
1.1 Topic Sentence
1.3 Use of past and present tense

1. Expectations for Student Work/Performance

Write at least one paragraph about our trip to Elkhorn Slough
- Introduce paragraph with appropriate topic sentence
- Capitalize first word of sentence and proper nouns
- Correctly use present and past tense

2. Students' Names

far below standard	approaching standard	meeting standard	exceeding standard
Jesse Matthew Teresa Lily Juan Chris	Melissa Tyrone Roberta Sara Tomas Vincente Loan Cody Dawn	Maggie Rachel Kevin Jackie Willie	
_30_ % of class	_45_ % of class	_25_ % of class	____ % of class

3. Description of Student Performance (one student from each category)

far below standard	approaching standard	meeting standard	exceeding standard
Teresa: • Simple topic sentence • 1 period at end of paragraph • present tense • Some caps at beginning of sentence	Cody: • Used model topic sentence • periods at end of all sentences • appropriate use of caps • sporadic correct use of past tense	Maggie: • Appropriate topic sentence • complete sentences • correct use of commas and periods • correct use of caps • correct past and present tense	

Source: © 2004 New Teacher Center at the University of California, Santa Cruz.

FIGURE 3-5 (continued)

ANALYSIS OF STUDENT WORK TOOL
PAGE 2

4. Learning Needs

far below standard	approaching standard	meeting standard	exceeding standard
Teresa: • Practice w/caps • understanding of tenses • Visuals of literacy concepts on walls • Practice writing sentences w/periods	Cody: • Practice writing topic sentences • Learn use of past tense	Maggie: • Increase richness of writing • Develop vocabulary • Challenged to publish writing	

5. Differentiated Strategies

Note any patterns and trends. Consider resources *and/or* personnel to support you.

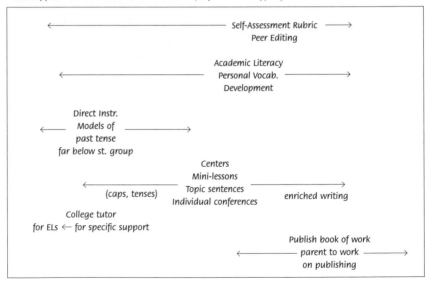

Source: © 2004 New Teacher Center at the University of California, Santa Cruz.

assignment. (Many teachers work so fast trying to create lesson plans and prepare for the next day that they omit the simple act of thinking about what they expect from students.)

The second prompt on the ASW asks new teachers to go through each student's assignment to identify to what extent the student met the articulated expectation or standard. The teacher then carefully reviews each piece of work and writes the names of students in the table to identify where they fall in meeting the standard. This is an imperfect process. Many new teachers will place students in areas that experienced teachers or mentors might not. Again, the goal is not to fill out the form correctly but rather to help new teachers understand the value of seeing that students are learning at different paces. As teachers' skills in this area develop, so will their ability to be more accurate in their assessments of learning needs.

Teachers are also asked to fill out the percentages of students within each category. Although bringing a calculator into the process might at first feel overly structured, it can be transformative as teachers realize, for example, that more than half the class did not meet the expectation for the assignment. This often opens many new teachers' eyes, helping them realize that their lesson was possibly not as effective as it could have been. More importantly, rather than assuming that it is the students' fault for not being engaged in the learning (an easy attitude to default to when things are not going well), it helps many teachers see their responsibility for ensuring that the lessons are delivered in ways that help all students understand and meet expectations.

The next prompt, "Description of Student Performance," asks teachers to go to a deeper level of analysis through a modified case-study approach. Taking one student from each identified level, the teacher describes, in conjunction with his mentor, what exactly it is about the student's work that caused him to place the student at that level. This action adds a significant layer of rigor to the process, because teachers are forced to use evidence and criteria for success in achieving the standard of a given skill or assignment. This thinking helps teachers move away from the tendency to place students in categories based on their general expectations of the child founded on experience (and other potential variables) and move toward an objective focus on whether the student is gaining the identified skill.

The third prompt, "Learning Needs," forces teachers to take the next critical step: identifying why the student selected in the modified case study is not achieving to standard and determining the next steps to be used to push those students who are learning at or above standard (a crucial and often overlooked component of teaching in urban public schools).

Finally, the culminating and most important piece of this process is the prompt "Differentiate Strategies," an activity that is based on the learning needs of each student in the room. This prompt forces teachers to change how they instruct individuals and groups of students based on the assessment of their learning needs. Although the ASW doesn't use the term "differentiated instruction," it helps new teachers to do just that: to modify their instructional strategies to meet the needs of each learner.

The expertise of mentors is extremely helpful in this part of the process. Few new teachers have a wide enough repertoire of instructional strategies to draw from and often become paralyzed when it comes to acting on the information in front of them. (Programs that seek to help teachers assess student learning often yield limited changes in practice, because they fail to bring in resources that help teachers take the next integral step of learning how to change instructional strategies to match the assessments.) Having mentors to provide ideas and brainstorm activities is therefore a critical piece in helping new teachers get over the hump of "what now?" and dive into the most important feature of teaching and learning: tailoring instruction to meet each student's needs.

The ASW is a practical tool for building new teacher skills in delivering effective instruction, and this exercise also provides an important opportunity to shape or shift a teacher's expectations of students. Through this assessment, many teachers learn that their pupils are not either good or bad students innately, but rather that each student has her own set of strengths and challenges that ebb and flow throughout the year. So, for example, a student who is acting up and falling behind during most of class might actually excel when it comes to acquiring a few key skills that other students are having a hard time with.

This kind of insight helps shine a light on each student during various parts of the year and reinforces the idea that all students can achieve to high standards if their learning needs and styles are understood and addressed. Such knowledge can push teachers the extra mile to identify the learning needs of those students whom they might otherwise have given up on; and importantly, it helps them understand how to differentiate instruction to push forward those who are already seeing success.

STRUCTURES FOR PROFESSIONAL DEVELOPMENT OF MENTORS

As the NTC works with programs such as those highlighted in this book, it supports the development of mentors in three essential ways:

- Mentor academies
- Mentor forums
- Mentor coaching and formative assessment

These interrelated structures offer opportunities for mentors to learn, integrate, and apply new knowledge and practices over time. Far beyond the brief introduction to mentoring most programs offer (the equivalent of a pre-service approach to mentor preparation), these professional learning environments support high-quality mentoring that advances teacher effectiveness, consistency of program implementation, and mentor accountability.

Mentor academies

Four times a year, NTC brings mentors together to participate in a learning community where they share information about best practices in developing relationships with new teachers, collecting and analyzing classroom and student data to inform practice, and assessing and supporting teacher growth and effectiveness. The two- to three-year academy curriculum is recursive, allowing opportunities for mentors to reflect on, practice, and build on what they have learned in earlier professional development sessions. The training introduces and builds skills over time as mentors' developmental needs typically emerge over the first few years of mentoring practice. Like new teachers, mentors benefit from a period of supported induction and ongoing professional development.

Mentor forums

Although the academies are an essential component of building one's knowledge of mentoring practice, the training is insufficient on its own. Creating communities of practice where mentors regularly meet to gain

---

NTC Mentor Academies

Year 1

Mentor Academy 1: Foundations in Mentoring and Formative Assessment Fundamental knowledge, skills, and understanding that are critical for those who work with beginning teachers.

Mentor Academy 2: Coaching and Observation Strategies Collection of observation data related to professional teaching standards and ways data can be shared to improve new teacher instructional practice.

Mentor Academy 3: Analysis of Student Work Principles of adult learning and strategies in coaching new teachers as they use student work to guide instructional planning.

Mentor Academy 4: Planning and Designing Professional Development for New Teachers Strategies to help bring new teachers together for meaningful and responsive learning

Year 2

Mentor Academy 5: Coaching in Complex Situations Formative assessment of mentors and building mentor capacity to engage successfully in difficult coaching conversations with beginning teachers.

Mentor Academy 6: Mentoring for Equity Framework for mentoring beginning teachers regarding issues related to race, language, and culture within the context of the professional teaching standards.

Mentor Academy 7: Artifacts of Practice Analysis of data of practice related to mentor formative assessment and programmatic improvement.

Mentor Academy 8: Teachers of Teachers Concepts and strategies to build mentor leadership skills to influence, impact, and advocate for mentoring.

---

insights into the work is critical to ensuring that mentors deepen their knowledge and build their capacity to be effective.

The NTC program therefore facilitates (or supports district program leaders in facilitating) a series of weekly mentor forums. These weekly forums give mentors an opportunity to digest the knowledge and skills learned in the academies, share best practices among colleagues, practice using tools and protocols to drive teacher practice forward, and identify ways of overcoming obstacles in the work. Figure 3-6 shows a sample agenda.

FIGURE 3-6 Sample mentor forum agenda

UNIVERSITY OF CALIFORNIA • SANTA CRUZ

Mentor Forum Agenda
October 25, 2002

8:30–9:15   **Connecting: Problem-Posing/Problem-Solving**
Purpose: To provide collegial support with mentoring challenges and concerns

9:15–9:25   **Review Agenda and Notes**
Recorder: John

9:25–10:30   **Learning: Checking for Systems of Equity**
Purpose: To practice using an observation tool that will support teaching for equity

10:30–10:45   **Break**

10:30–11:00   **Learning continued: Teacher Expectations and Student Achievement**
Purpose: To refine our understanding about how teacher expectations impact student achievement

11:00–11:15   **Business/Announcements**
- Beginning Teacher Consent forms due
- Upcoming Workshops:
    10/30 Coaching in Complex Situations
    11/20 Using Technology: Classroom Management Course

11:15–11:30   **Closing: Reflections, 3–2–1**

Next Meeting: Nov. 2, 2002
Refreshments: Tim, Sandra, Rose
Public Recorder: Diane

Source: © 2004 New Teacher Center at the University of California, Santa Cruz.

The conversations are always inquiry based and grounded in data about the new teachers whom mentors are working with so that mentors can accurately reflect on their experiences in the field and support the development of their own practice. When done well, these conversations provide a model framework for professional learning communities that support instructional rigor, collaboration, focused learning, and intellectual engagement at the highest levels.

This developmental, responsive, data-driven, and recursive approach to training is aligned with the type of support NTC believes teachers themselves need if they are to succeed in the classroom, and similarly the type of support students need to thrive. By modeling these types of rigorous conversations with mentors, the program provides increased opportunities to inform and facilitate similar conversations among and between educators in schools and, although often overlooked, among leaders within central district administration.

Mentor coaching and formative assessment

The third element in the NTC program of mentor professional development is the practice of linking each mentor with a peer coach within a structured process of mentor formative assessment. Mentors gain personal experience with a systematic and collaborative formative assessment process supported by a coaching partnership. These structures and protocols, designed specifically for the mentors, mimic the FAS tools and processes used with new teachers, including a set of mentor standards and a continuum of mentor development.

Coaching partners meet regularly and schedule opportunities to observe and collect data of each mentor's practice in an identified area for professional growth. By engaging in a cycle of continuous improvement, mentors learn and practice the behaviors they are striving to foster in the new teachers. Coaching partners help cement these behaviors throughout the mentor community and strengthen the vision and promise of the mentoring program.

TEACHING THE TEACHERS

The ultimate effectiveness of an instructional mentoring program depends on the skills of those who serve as mentors. As a result, the NTC has elected to focus a great deal of its work on the development of these teachers of teachers, who have the potential to positively affect the growth and effectiveness of their less experienced colleagues. NTC's program of professional development for mentors is extensive and complex and interweaves the principles of continuous professional improvement with effective instruction for all students.

In each of the case studies that follow, the districts chose to use most elements of NTC's approach to mentor development as an important foundational component of their program implementation. The NTC mentor curriculum served as a touchstone for these programs, helping accelerate the mentors' development while conveying key principles and practices in support of new teacher effectiveness. The cases highlight how districts have worked to create the programmatic context in which these mentors, their new teachers, and those teachers' students can thrive.

PART II

The Case Studies

4
—

Durham Public Schools

At the core of learning is the classroom teacher. Teachers, by and large, have the greatest struggles during their first few years on the job. In order to keep those teachers, we must give them support . . . And our new teachers know they have a master teacher that they can rely on.

—Carl Harris, superintendent, Durham Public Schools

BACKGROUND AND PROGRAM DESIGN

Durham Public Schools (DPS) is a medium-sized urban school district in North Carolina, located just outside Raleigh, the state's capital. (See box, "State Policy Context.") The district has approximately thirty-three thousand students. On average, nearly 50 percent of students qualify for free or reduced-price lunches.

Before implementation of the new mentoring program, Durham suffered from one of the highest teacher attrition rates in the state. The district struggled to recruit new teachers, and several local universities were less than enthusiastic about placing student teachers in some Durham schools. After reviewing teacher mobility trends, district leadership determined that more than a quarter of new teachers were leaving the school system every year.

The following case describes Durham's efforts to implement a high-quality mentoring program to address issues of not only attrition but also teacher effectiveness.

Mentor ratios and matching

The Durham Public Schools mentoring program releases mentors full-time from their classroom positions to support first-, second-, and third-year teachers throughout the district. Implemented in 2005, the program employs thirty-five carefully selected full-time mentors and a part-time director. Mentors serve for three years and then rotate back to the classroom or go on to other leadership positions in the district.

The model differs from the typical New Teacher Center program in that the mentors are not limited to working with teachers of a specific subject and work primarily in one or two schools, with a handful of mentors working in three schools. Each mentor assists approximately eighteen new teachers per year, with the amount of support generally based on the teacher's experience level. First-year teachers typically receive the most mentoring time, second-year teachers a moderate amount of time, and third-year teachers the least.

Given that most mentors were assigned to one school and in the belief that third-year teachers require less of a mentor's time, DPS has elected to increase the ratio of beginning teachers to mentors beyond the NTC-recommended 15:1. Many mentors also choose to work occasionally with their new teachers in groups, developing collaborative learning environments among cohorts of new teachers who work in the same school. Other groups include pairings of new teachers with veteran teachers of the same subject and grade level. Additionally, mentors visit other school sites as needed to support new teacher practice in their areas of expertise. This policy mitigates some of the pedagogical limitations encountered by mentor generalists when working across subjects.

Mentor training

For the first three years of the program, all mentors participated in NTC's Mentor Academy series, a three-year professional development program facilitated by NTC staff. Through these sessions, mentors learned how to (1) develop their mentoring skills, (2) use professional teaching standards to focus teacher development, and (3) use formative assessment to guide the instructional growth of new teachers and nurture teacher excellence. With NTC support, DPS program leadership instituted biweekly mentor forums to build a professional learning community for mentors.

State Policy Context

North Carolina requires that all first-, second-, and third-year teachers receive mentoring support. Districts receive $1,000 per first- and second-year teacher to support mentoring. For many years, the state board of education has recommended that full-time mentor programs be funded in all districts.

A state-level Mentoring Task Force was convened to explore the feasibility of supporting full-time programs as well as exploring opportunities to assess current mentoring activities, develop comprehensive mentor program standards, and determine potential legislative and funding opportunities for improving programs throughout the state.

A unique feature of North Carolina's policies is the acknowledgment of the working conditions of new teachers, including the tendency to assign beginning teachers "the most difficult students, multiple preparations, and multiple extra-curricular assignments."[a] The state asserts, "These working conditions prohibit on-the-job learning and negatively influence teacher job satisfaction" and strongly recommends that new teachers be assigned in their area of licensure, be provided a mentor early, and be assigned limited preparations, limited noninstructional duties, limited exceptional or difficult students, and no extracurricular activities (unless requested in writing).

[a]"Policies on the Beginning Teacher Support Program," North Carolina State Board of Education Policy Manual, QP-A-004 (August 2006).

Over the three years of the program, NTC staff has worked to build the capacity of the program leaders (director and identified mentor leaders) to learn and facilitate the training component of the program. This process has enabled the NTC to step back from the role of external professional development provider while continuing to serve as a thought partner and critical friend of the district.

Senior-level collaboration

In 2005, Durham district leaders initiated conversations about changing the way they inducted new teachers into the system. At the time, it was acknowledged that some pockets of the school community were providing new teachers with meaningful support, but high-level support was generally idiosyncratic, based on particular personalities or circumstance.

To help her decide how the district would engage in this effort to revamp new teacher induction, Ann Denlinger, then superintendent, requested that members of the executive leadership team attend an NTC Induction Institute. The composition of the institute team was unique in that it included senior leaders from human resources, staff development, operations, recruitment and retention, secondary education, and elementary education.

The Durham team's sense of purpose set it apart from the other teams. DPS attendees stayed late in the afternoons, held meetings after dinner, drew the NTC facilitators in to their discussions to answer questions, and returned each morning with yet another piece of the emerging program puzzle in place. At the end of the week the team boarded the plane back home with a multifaceted and comprehensive plan of action.

The decision to send leaders from multiple departments was the first critical building block. Each team member had the time to listen to the research, practices, policies, and philosophies that underpin high-quality mentoring, and each was able to understand how such a program might support his own particular initiatives and outcomes. Leaders from human resources and operations saw the potential to use mentoring as leverage for increasing teacher retention, and leaders from primary/secondary education, staff development, and curriculum and instruction viewed the program as an opportunity to align instructional strategies and support current initiatives to build professional learning communities.

One district leader commented, "We all got it. We got that it could help each of us do what we needed to do . . . and we got that it would be better, stronger, if we did it together." Once the team of district leaders understood how the NTC model could support their own initiatives, they developed a shared sense of purpose and decided to move forward with collective ownership of the initiative.

Funding

The DPS team members were determined to find funding to support this ambitious initiative even though they weren't sure where the funding would come from. At about the same time, the district undertook a fiscal review focused on streamlining educational operations to free up dollars to be used in the classroom. By aligning programs, the group located significant funding. Many of the funds came from Title II funds that were thought either to be redundant or not to support the intent of the entitlement (supporting teacher recruitment and retention).

The district was also challenged by a North Carolina state policy that allocates $1,000 per beginning teacher to be used as a stipend for mentors. With a full-release mentoring model, DPS leaders would not be paying the mentors an additional stipend, but there was no provision for these funds to be collapsed into a lump sum to support alternative models of mentoring. The district successfully petitioned the state policy makers for a waiver that would enable DPS to pool these funds to support its vision of full-release mentoring.

Both the former and the current superintendents knew that funding was not necessarily easy to find, nor maintain, and that some tough decisions would have to be made. But Superintendent Carl Harris said, "When others ask me, 'How can you afford to do something like this?' I say, 'It's a priority.' . . . At the core of teaching and learning is a highly qualified teacher, and we can't get there unless we make that a priority."

The superintendent knew that the district had a cadre of leaders who shared this vision and would champion the program.

Communication

The collective ownership of the mentoring task force, along with the superintendent's strong advocacy, raised the profile and prestige of the initiative. When news spread of the coming program, all members of the school system's community knew it was a top priority for district leaders. In the fall of 2005, Denlinger used the opening of school as a strategic opportunity to address and convey her priorities to the entire DPS administrator community. She highlighted the district's new teacher mentoring program and invited NTC's executive director, Ellen Moir, to share key insights about the program alongside her.

The district leaders on the task force also made it a top priority to ensure that information about the program was shared with school leaders even before its implementation. They anticipated push-back from principals who would be asked to give up some of their top educators to serve as mentors. The leaders decided to address this concern head-on by spearheading a series of information sessions for principals in which they articulated the goals and vision of the program.

In these sessions, district leaders explained the program and stressed the shift from short-term gains for individual schools to long-term gains for students throughout the system. Although some principals remained skeptical of, or even resistant to, the idea of losing their best educators, many bought in to the values of the program and the impact it could have on students systemwide. Some felt these sessions were a turning point. One principal recalls a huge turnaround in her thinking about the program:

> When I heard about the program, I thought it was the dumbest thing I ever heard. Why are you going to take some of the best thirty teachers out of the classroom? This is a huge chunk of assets to our kids . . . but I was wrong. I was dead wrong. When I came into the principalship, to be the instructional leader, as hard as I have tried, I don't have the time to do what I know needs to get done. [My mentor] has the time—and the expertise to move those teachers forward . . . she's being an instructional leader.

Another principal echoed this sentiment, saying, "[My mentor] can get in that classroom more than I can. She doesn't make judgments; she makes suggestions for improvement. She's able to understand what the learning needs are and gets them the information right away. She focuses on the task at the time, which I can't do often."

Although many principals became convinced of the program's potential, some of them continued to be doubtful. After watching dozens of programs and district and state mandates fly in and out of the school doors, these principals were (understandably) suspicious of any new initiative that sought substantive reform. This issue was aggravated, another principal said, "because the selection process was so strong. They were indeed taking the *best* teachers out of the schools." Where the messages got across about the need to think systemwide, as opposed to only schoolwide, principal engagement was deeper—though not perfect. However, the percentage of principals who were resistant to the program was significantly smaller than in many districts where limited or no principal engagement took place.

Mentor selection

With a significant portion of principals on board and a solid commitment from the superintendent and senior DPS leaders, members of the task force knew they were in a strong position to hire some of the best and brightest educators to serve as mentors. They set the selection bar extremely high and developed a policy that prioritized quality over quantity.

They began by using the NTC guidelines, mentor selection criteria, and accompanying rubric, which outline the critical qualities of instructional mentors. To this, they added the expectation that every mentor candidate should have a solid track record of instructional excellence and consistently high student test scores to prove it. Furthermore, program leaders decided not to hire anyone who did not meet the high standards they set. If a sufficient number of applicants did not meet their high expectations, they would modify the program to work with a smaller number.

This decision was evidence of leadership's commitment to ensure a cadre of mentors that represented some of the top educators in the system and sent a message to the district community that program quality was a top priority. The selected teachers were true master educators, and as a result they stepped into their mentor role having the skills they needed not only to succeed in the work but also to win over the school staff in ways that proved that they were invaluable assets and critical resources for the school community. In other words, the quality of the mentors validated the need for the program.

This success significantly aided the first year of implementation, especially compared with other district programs where mentors had to build a reputation of quality after years of development and outreach. Working with high-caliber mentors also meant that the community of practice among mentors was exceptional and accelerated the rate of mentor growth, allowing more new teachers to thrive sooner in their careers. The high quality of mentors cannot be understated in the success of the implementation.

School-based, generalist approach

Durham program leaders have initiated a generalist approach to mentoring. This means that mentors are not matched with new teachers by subject area, even though there is research suggesting that subject-matter matching is a key element of programs that have strong outcomes. Rather, DPS leaders focused on matching mentors with schools. Each mentor works in one or two schools, supporting all first-, second-, and third-year teachers.

By serving teachers in a range of subject areas and multiple grade levels, mentors are pushed outside their areas of expertise.

Interestingly, mentors themselves credit this as one of the most important factors in the program's success. "It forced us to become learners—and to rely on the expertise of our colleagues," one mentor notes. Mentors turned to one another to fill gaps in their knowledge. Those mentors with an expertise in English turned to those with an expertise in math, math teachers turned to art teachers, and so on.

Not only do the mentors extend their knowledge into new subject areas, but they also became facilitators of intervisitations. In these visitations, mentors work with other mentors to arrange for new teachers to visit classrooms of strong, experienced teachers, where they can observe, collect data, and reflect on and analyze the practice they observe. One mentor suggests that the collaboration among their community, and within the school context, creates a seamless team approach that broadens the support for new teachers. She asserts, "Sometimes when I'm talking with a new teacher, I can't address the issue . . . but I can get her someone that can."

These school-based mentors also develop a strong knowledge of the schools where they serve and build deep relationships with principals. When the mentors' work is focused on only one or two sites, they are likely to be seen as part of the school community. Principals seem to have a better sense of what the mentors are doing, and this enables them to identify other ways in which the mentors might impact instruction throughout the school.

For example, some principals have asked mentors to open up professional development opportunities for other teachers in the school or share strategies that support collaborative learning environments. Other principals have used the mentor as a critical friend to help plan training, assess implementation of various initiatives, or identify strategies for targeted support of specific teachers. One principal uses his mentor to better inform his own efforts to improve instruction:

> My job is to create an atmosphere that people want to be in. [My mentor] lets me know when someone needs extra attention or needs to use a product that can support their instruction. She can tell me where to be, and when, and even how to approach the teacher sometimes, because you know they

all come with different styles, and baggage, and I want to be doing things that are going to be supportive and not detrimental . . . and she helps me to do that.

Not all DPS administrators feel this strongly about their mentors, but teacher and principal buy in is stronger than in other programs NTC has partnered with over the years. Mentor efforts continue to focus on supporting new teacher development, but in the regular course of their work mentors often extend their efforts to the entire school community.

At one school site, the mentor brings together her new teachers each week to engage in a professional community of practice where they address areas of concern, share ideas, review student work, or discuss new instructional strategies. She has found that after the new teachers complete their mentoring experience, many want to continue to participate in these weekly gatherings. The group has expanded to include some veteran staff members and is beginning to contribute to the design and facilitation of staff meetings. Not only are the new teachers developing leadership capacity, but also the mentor has been able to support the principal in welcoming teacher input and shared ownership of the faculty meetings. Such examples suggest that the decision to create a school-focused program with generalist mentors is an interesting one and certainly worthy of further exploration.

The generalist model may also be particularly attractive to districts that do not have enough numbers of new teachers in each subject area to warrant a full-time mentor in that area. Only massive city districts can implement subject-specific mentors with ease. The Durham experience shows that the generalist model has merit, and that sort of model is generalizable to most districts around the country.

Collaborative professional communities of practice

From the start, DPS adopted the NTC model of bringing mentors together on a regular basis (in Durham's case, bimonthly) for three- to four-hour mentor meetings focused on building a community of practice, deepening the mentors' learning, and accelerating the mentors' development. Led by program director Fred Williams, these mentor forums are an important component of Durham's program. Mentors credit Williams with creating a supportive, stimulating environment where mentors learn from one another in a safe and engaging context; Williams credits the high caliber of mentors and their intellectual curiosity as the reasons for such high-performing collaborative activity.

In any case, Durham mentor program forums (a component of the NTC plan for ongoing professional development) provide examples of best practices in collaborative learning. One district leader asserts that these forums are the "best example of professional learning communities" anywhere in the system. Characterized by the use of data, analysis of student work, inquiry, professional norms, creativity, and intellectual rigor, these forums provide a platform that supports mentor development, improved beginning teacher practice, and school and district program improvement strategies.

Mentors are positioned well to support districtwide reform for two reasons: stature and timing. Because they are master educators and have the support of senior leaders, these individuals are seen as important resources and therefore serve as critical thought partners with school and district leaders.

Mentors are learning how to design and sustain a rich, dynamic community of practice in which they are learners as well as leaders, and this experience carries over to their schools. A recent districtwide effort to implement professional learning communities (PLCs) has coincided with the mentoring program, providing an entry point for mentors to work with school teams in meaningful ways.

Many of the mentors have begun working with their new teachers in groups, mimicking the type of reflection- and inquiry-based conversations that have been modeled for them in mentor forums. This practice enables new teachers to learn from one another and builds a sense of shared purpose and community that otherwise might not have been present. One principal says that as a result of this work, "our newer teachers in their second and third years are more confident and quicker to jump into leadership roles. Our third-year teachers are helping the first-year teachers, and second-year teachers are cross-pollinating their ideas with other teachers across the grade levels. And this was all modeled by the mentor in the first place."

The PLC initiative has led to efforts to increase the number and quality of collaborative meetings in schools (such as cross-disciplinary, grade-level, and teacher-experience-level meetings), and principals see their mentors as important resources who can help address knowledge gaps in how to implement such communities. Mentors are invited to critical conversations about instruction, often to guide the effort. Whether issued by the teachers mentors are working with, or by administrators or veteran teachers in the schools they support, these invitations serve as vehicles for linking student- and classroom-level observation data with school-level conversations about practice. Further, having honed their skills and knowledge for building teacher capacity through inquiry and reflection, mentors are perceived as key levers for developing and maintaining robust professional learning communities.

Principal engagement

With all the key pieces in place—senior-level support, rigorous selection of mentors, a school-focused approach, and a concerted effort to bring administrators on board—it seems as though the district would be a model for developing principal ownership of the mentoring initiative. Although the district's approach has far exceeded that of many other districts and many principals seem to be using mentors as critical resources, the program has not reached its goal of full buy in from all administrators.

Program leaders cite principal buy in as one of the greatest challenges they face. Some administrators are not aware of the role of the mentor in the school or do not understand how the mentor's efforts support beginning teachers and student learning. A few issues impede full buy in. One is related to principal attrition. Although program leaders made great efforts to bring principals on board during the program's inception, many school leaders have since left their positions. Further efforts are needed to build the new principals' knowledge of the program to strengthen their support.

Another issue is related to mentor–principal matching. Many of the principals who have outstanding relationships with their mentors credit it to a strong match in work style, personality, and vision. One principal notes, "I never expected my relationship with [my mentor] to be as productive and strong as it is. I think a lot of it has to do with [my mentor]. A lot of it has to do with our personalities. We work well together." When principals perceive their mentors as being well matched with them in these areas, the relationship evolves into a strong, team-based approach that supports instructional excellence.

When principals do not have the same degree of rapport with their mentors, however, the result might be a certain degree of mistrust or skepticism about the program. Although the mentor might be doing great work with the new teachers, a mismatch in personalities or modus operandi can lead to conflicting approaches or information given to the new teacher. This discrepancy often confuses or overwhelms the new teacher, potentially leading to increased frustration—and may, in fact, exacerbate attrition.

Durham mentors suggest that one of the most powerful contributors to developing meaningful relationships with principals is time. The first year of the program and of the mentor's development at a given school site might be bumpy, as principal and mentor forge a relationship and begin to learn about each other's work. But by the third year, principals seem to better understand the mentors' role and are more likely to appreciate them as reliable resources principals can draw on to meet their schools' instructional goals. In addition, because each school has only one mentor (as opposed to programs in other districts, where schools may have several mentors), principals are not splitting their time to learn about the work of multiple mentors—only the one that they've grown a relationship with over time.

Systemic alignment

Durham public schools began their mentoring initiative with strong collaboration and a shared vision throughout the divisions. Leaders housed the program under the Department of Human Resources, recognizing that this initiative was about building human capital. Task force leaders from all departments remained part of the initiative and capitalized on opportunities for collaboration wherever feasible.

For example, the senior director of professional growth and development regularly attends the biweekly mentor forums. This provides a feedback loop that helps senior leaders understand what mentors are learning in the field and what new teachers need, and it helps shape future initiatives for professional development.

However, even though the interest in and commitment to collaboration have been consistently high, there has not been sufficient time to implement collaborative activities. In addition to the initial development of the program (identifying resources, mentor selection reviews) and participation at mentor forums, the district has had limited success in aligning mentor strategies under the HR Department with strategies coming from staff development, curriculum and instruction, and instructional technology. Leaders from all departments cite a strong will to collaborate but a lack of time to focus on what collaboration might look like. In the absence of this collaboration, HR has primarily led the charge on program implementation and monitoring.

Leaders report that even though collaboration and alignment have occurred at the school level between mentors and other key instructional staff (such as curriculum developers), these examples are isolated and idiosyncratic. There have been limited efforts to align the support strategies in a systematic and strategic way.

Some leaders suggest that, as a result, new educational initiatives are being implemented without adequate exposure to mentors. The three-year rotation helps address this issue, but mentors often have limited knowledge of the newest curriculum and instruction strategies. Even when mentors pick up the basics of new initiatives, generally they have little time to identify the nuances of seamlessly aligning support strategies.

As a result, some leaders fear that new teachers may be confused or overwhelmed by conflicting messages or overlapping frameworks. Leaders are exploring the idea of training mentors in all new instructional initiatives, but they fear that this time-consuming measure might take away from the time mentors spend with new teachers. One district leader asserts, "We know mentors need to be exposed to curriculum . . . and curriculum directors need to be trained in pedagogy and coaching strategies. The only thing inhibiting this piece is the time issue. I'd love to do that . . . it's important. But tell me when."

Impact data

DPS is examining a variety of data related to program impact, including new teacher retention, student learning, and teacher efficacy. A few key pieces of information have begun to emerge from district efforts to review outcomes. HR personnel conducted an Initial Licensure Report for the state and found significant improvement in teacher retention, reducing attrition by half during the first three years of the program. Specifically, from 2000 to 2005, the turnover rate for first-, second-, and third-year teachers averaged about 28 percent. In the first year of the program (2005–2006), turnover was reduced to 18 percent, and by 2007–2008 (the program's third year) turnover had dropped to 14 percent. District leaders continue to review teacher mobility data to determine trends over time.

School officials have also begun to look at how the program affects student achievement. In the absence of experimental design and value-added methodology, it is difficult to establish causal relationships. However, district leaders have found promising indicators of success. An internal district comparison looked at the differences in student test scores between students of veteran teachers and students of beginning teachers being supported by mentors. In areas containing the highest numbers of beginning teachers (Algebra I, Algebra II, Geometry, and English I)—where comparisons can be claimed most generalizable—new teachers showed student achievement gains as great as (or significantly greater than) their more-experienced peers.

This comparison does not account for student population background, teacher assignment, or other potential contributing factors. However, much research suggests that new teachers in their first few years on the job make the lowest gains in student achievement. Thus, the internal DPS report offers promising signals that a strong mentoring program may significantly accelerate the instructional progress of new teachers. More research is needed to validate these findings and determine which factors are helping these teachers most in terms of their success.

CONCLUDING OBSERVATIONS

It has been inspiring to see the development of Durham's program over the past four years. During the 2007–2008 school year, the NTC supported mentors in an inquiry process that engaged them in studying and collecting data on their program, their mentoring, and their new teachers. NTC followed those inquiry projects and saw an impressive professional learning community in action. In May 2008, teams of mentors shared their questions and their findings. Superintendent Carl Harris joined the group and shared his insights and his own research on beginning teachers. Several visitors commented that they had never seen such a remarkable level of discourse and rich learning.

Each year the program has gotten better, in part because of the developmental nature of implementing a program and in part because of the reflective nature of the program leader and the mentors. NTC has interviewed the mentors each year to better understand their learning and their career trajectories. Mentors come in as great teachers and leave as great teachers of teachers. Durham's district leaders report that their district has become a destination for new teachers; area colleges and universities are eagerly sending their graduates to teach in Durham, and colleagues from Durham are helping the state department of education and the board of education design mentoring policies that support teacher development and student learning.

LESSONS LEARNED

The program in Durham represents a slight divergence from the typical NTC model. A number of new learnings have resulted from its innovative trajectory, providing promising new strategies for supporting new teachers, and schools, in ways that may significantly improve outcomes for teachers and kids. Other learnings expose important questions about teaching and learning that compel us to look deeper into the work and ultimately to think more strategically about how we engage in the work in the future.

Creating an excellent mentor recruitment and selection process

The Durham leadership team realized early on that selecting exemplary teachers to serve as mentors was the single most important aspect of the mentoring initiative. The team led a vigorous recruitment campaign and followed it with a rigorous selection process.

Most importantly, the selection process was sanctioned and advocated by leadership across the system. Communication from the superintendent to leaders in human resources and teaching and learning made it clear that this position was a top priority. This endorsement gave mentoring the prestige to attract high-quality candidates.

In addition to an interview protocol and other application-related requirements, the leadership decided to review all candidates' student achievement records, ensuring that outstanding levels of instruction were evidenced. Many systems are not in a position, politically or logistically, to engage in this type of approach.

Finally, Durham leaders set the bar high and refused to lower it under any circumstances. When faced with the option of either hiring educators who did not meet their rigorous standards or being understaffed, the program chose to be understaffed. Although this decision is arguable, it sent a strong message to the district that only exceptional educators were being recruited for the position.

These recruitment and selection strategies are important levers for implementing high-quality programs. In many other systems, high-quality educators do not necessarily apply in the initial year, because many assume that the program is transitory or ancillary. These systems therefore miss out on a core population of educators who might otherwise propel the mentoring program to great success early in its implementation. However, when district leadership provides the platform to sanction mentors as true master educators—with all the merit and prestige it deserves—a program can become a draw for the best educators in the system. By setting the bar high and refusing to lower standards to meet quantitative goals, leaders send the message that this program is different from any other and helps attract the high-quality candidates who are inspired by efforts to bring excellence to education.

Sustainable structures for collaboration and alignment

Durham leaders are seeking to stagger mentor rotations so that a cadre of mentor leaders is always available to support new mentors, building their skills and knowledge, and new mentors are always available to teach new teachers about recent initiatives. Although this structure seeks to support increased awareness of and alignment with new initiatives, it has fallen short of the desired goal. Without an explicit process for showing links between current initiatives and mentoring, mentors often have difficulty trying to connect their work with the latest professional development efforts in schools. District leaders and mentors alike are interested in addressing this gap in knowledge, but because of logistical and budgetary boundaries they have not yet defined structures that can meet this need.

Additionally, one of the flagship initiatives in the district focuses on building collaborative professional learning communities. Mentors have occasionally helped shape and sometimes have spearheaded these efforts in schools, but such work has been idiosyncratic. By analyzing where and why these practices are thriving, district leaders can build on the success and replicate the process throughout the district.

Mentor–teacher matching

As mentioned earlier, the Durham program assigns mentors to specific schools and does not match mentors and beginning teachers based on content expertise. The district compensates for what might be a knowledge gap by ensuring the selection of high-quality mentors and then providing them with extensive ongoing professional development. Whether this development occurs through facilitating intervisitations, building mentors' own knowledge of subject areas outside their expertise, or focusing on classroom data that address pedagogy, it appears that lack of content matching has not compromised the mentors' work; in fact, it may have enhanced its effectiveness.

The apparent success of this approach mitigates research that suggests subject-matter matching is an integral component of mentoring programs. One explanation for the apparent discrepancy is that such research tends to review traditional or nonrigorous programs, where the quality of mentor selection and training are low. In these programs, mentors may have only a basic understanding of how to approach mentoring and may adopt a let-me-tell-you-what-I-know approach. This strategy may be more effective when the mentor has information about the same subject and grade area, but often it does not provide a yield in deep capacity building of new teacher practice.

Durham's extremely rigorous selection process and training program mean that mentor caliber is extremely high, allowing mentors to reach beyond their own areas of expertise.

Limiting the number of schools and mentor–principal matching

Mentors work in either one, two, or (rarely) three schools. As a result, they are in a great position to acquire in-depth knowledge of the school's

culture, develop strong relationships with the administrators, and identify ways to inform (and be informed by) school strategies for professional
development. This arrangement allows mentors to be seen as a part of
the school community. It also builds their credibility and loyalty to each
school setting and enhances their ability to tailor their support plans for
each new teacher to the needs and context of the school.

Interestingly, most of the principals themselves did not participate in the
mentor selection process, but many principals acknowledge that the time
they've had to connect with the mentor over a number of years has significantly improved their working relationship and outcomes. This information has recently been reinforced by research suggesting that a mentor's
familiarity with a school setting has a significant impact on attrition rates.

This information is important for new programs. In many settings, full-
time mentors will work in more than four or five schools at a time, typically
because program directors want to maximize the number of subject-matter
matches. (A mentor with a larger number of subject-matter matches in her
caseload generally serves in a greater number of schools.) However, it seems
as though the benefits of having mentors serve in only one or two schools
might outweigh some of the costs associated with having fewer subject-
matter matches, especially when the caliber of mentors is particularly high.

It is important to note that the mentor–principal relationship has not
worked out in some cases. Some DPS principals suggest that differences
in work style, personalities, or instructional support approaches have created rifts between principals and mentors. These differences make it challenging to implement the program, and the time between mentor and new
teacher potentially is diminished or diluted.

When program leaders look at assigning mentors to schools, they might
benefit from taking the extra step to review matches between mentors
and principals. They might also consider developing structures that allow
for new assignments if relationships are not developing well between the
matched pairs.

Capacity and alignment

Consistent with what the NTC has seen in many district programs, one of
the continuing challenges in the Durham district is the pace of new initia-

tives. This rate of change challenges mentors, who are responsible for supporting teacher effectiveness in the context of these innovations. Districts must confront how to build the capacity of mentors so that they are on top of these changes. The need for time, funding, and coordination complicates the efforts.

One DPS district leader suggests an interesting solution to this issue. If a district leader, partner institutions, or identified mentors themselves could isolate the pieces of training that are most relevant to the work of the mentors and help make concrete links between emerging initiatives and mentor protocols, then the work could be more strategically aligned and the information gap addressed.

Ongoing communication with principals

Building strong collaborative partnerships with principals is an essential component of a high-quality mentoring experience. Durham's school-focused approach helps strengthen the working relationship between mentors and principals across the board. Yet program leaders continue to talk about the need to further develop administrator buy in and still occasionally encounter principals who do not understand the program or do not feel as if they have ownership of it.

One obstacle to full administrator buy in has been principal turnover. Although district leaders attempted to bring principals on board during program initiation, new principals coming in have little or no awareness of those activities. In addition, because the intensity of communication about the program has understandably diminished a bit over four years, principals' interest and excitement about the program may have plateaued. Some suggest that most of the principals are now so accustomed to this support that they inherently rely on it.

Mentors are also responsible for engaging principals regularly. When the mentor and the principal are aligned and focused on a set of goals and outcomes, beginning teachers and their students will have the greatest success. Yet many experienced teachers may need support in learning how to communicate effectively with school leaders—even their own. Sometimes, when the program maintains a separation between supervision and mentoring, the mentor may be uncertain how to maintain confidentiality.

If principal engagement is to be sustained over time, districts should consider developing structures that maintain regular communication with new as well as veteran administrators and identify methods for maintaining program momentum. Methods might include holding ongoing breakfast meetings with administrators, inviting administrators to specific training or forums, or even asking new teachers to share with principals some of the things they've learned from their work with mentors.

5

Boston Public Schools

Our campaign to build a strong human capital strategy in our schools is—at its heart—a campaign to ensure that all adults in our schools have the skills and knowledge they need to help kids succeed. Supporting our newest teachers is paramount to realizing success in this effort.

—*Carol Johnson, superintendent, Boston Public Schools*

MENTORING PROGRAM BACKGROUND

The Boston Public Schools (BPS) mentor program emerged from a number of influences. District leaders, local and national foundations, unions, and advocacy organizations helped create the entry point for building this program. While many diverse forces paved the way, it was not necessarily a straight road. (See box, "State Policy Context.")

The origin might be linked to the focus of former superintendent Tom Payzant, who implemented a human capital strategy. During his tenure, Payzant worked on many facets of the system to enhance and develop the skills and talents of school practitioners. One element of this strategy, which came in the latter part of his tenure, was a revamping of the Office of Human Resources (HR) to better support new teachers, who were estimated to be leaving the system at the startling rate of 50 percent in the first three years of teaching (compared with a national rate of approximately 33 percent).[1]

State Policy Context

Massachusetts has approved state regulations that require first-year educators to complete a one-year induction program with a mentor. Guidelines encourage districts to incorporate state standards into mentoring programs, including an orientation, a trained mentor, a support team including mentor and administrator, and release time for the mentor and new teacher to engage in mentoring activities. Funding has not been appropriated to support consistent statewide implementation.

As with many other urban systems, HR faced many challenges, including antiquated data systems, layers of well-entrenched bureaucracy, late and cumbersome hiring procedures, and slow responsiveness to schools and educators. The Boston Plan for Excellence (BPE), a local education foundation that partners with BPS to provide research and strategy on reform initiatives, conducted a study in 2002–2003, finding that 65 percent of new teachers rated the support from the Office of Human Resources as "poor" or "fair."[2] Additional anecdotal information about the gaps in services reinforced this data. One internal staff person observed, "Schools would literally have to try and earn credits . . . build favor with staff in the [HR] office so that they might have a chance of getting a decent staff person. It was completely dysfunctional . . . and just wasn't [assigning teachers] based on where the best teachers were needed."

Payzant's intent was to shift this paradigm. To do this, he brought in a Fellow with the Broad Superintendent's Academy (a program of the Broad Center for the Management of School Systems designed to support capacity building of potential leaders in education) as an assistant superintendent to reinvent HR. One of the assistant superintendent's primary initiatives in this process was to make the office more oriented toward customer service so that schools and teachers were viewed as clients that HR was working to support—and not the other way around. The metaphor the assistant superintendent often used, and that resonated throughout the district, was that she wanted to "roll out the red carpet for all new teachers from contact to contract." From the first day they applied to the day they signed their contract, she wanted to create a seamless, positive experience that would make teachers feel welcome, knowledgeable, and confident.

With the help of a number of national and local foundations, including the Broad Foundation, the Dell Foundation, the Harold Whitworth Pierce Charitable Trust, Strategic Grant Partners, Barr Foundation, and a cadre of leaders within the system, the assistant superintendent successfully mobilized a reform effort that inspired a new way of business and transformed the HR system. A subsequent BPE 2007–2008 survey of new teachers found that the number of teachers reporting that the support they received from HR was either poor or fair had dropped to 21 percent (from 65 percent), and the number reporting that the support they received from HR was good or excellent had risen to 63 percent (from 16 percent).[3]

Although the isolated impact on teacher satisfaction is not known, a number of strategies may have contributed to the turnaround, including a streamlined, online application process, paperwork assistance, follow-up support, and a newly designed teacher preparation program called the Boston Teacher Residency (BTR) program, developed as an initiative of the Boston Plan for Excellence in partnership with the Boston Public Schools.[4]

It was perceived that all these initiatives were significantly improving the experience and quality of new teachers coming to BPS for the first time. However, district leaders quickly became aware that even though the operational outcomes of their efforts were successful, not all new teachers were receiving the type of support for teaching and learning that would help them be most effective.

There was widespread acknowledgment that the existing teacher mentoring program was implemented inconsistently and had a number of challenges. Like many traditional programs, the Boston program had limitations on the selection of mentors and time for interactions between mentors and beginning teachers, including limited time for observation of practice. In addition, mentors generally received little or no professional development, a factor that one report states was "limiting [mentors'] own growth as well as their capacity to influence the practice of their mentees."[5]

When data came out showing that the first cohort of BTR teachers also cited a lack of support, the district took action and sought out a new type of mentoring. However, the district did not have funding for a new, fully developed program for all new teachers at that time.

Fortuitously, BPS came across some new dollars provided by an external entity, which provided the opportunity to pilot a new, more robust mentoring program using full-time release mentors to support a subset of first-year elementary teachers. The district adopted significant measures to identify and select outstanding candidates to be mentors. Officials also were careful to prioritize time for interactions between mentors and new teachers and facilitate mentors' and beginning teachers' professional development.

Positive responses from principals, new teachers, and mentors created enthusiasm and excitement that resonated in a number of circles within the district and led to a proposal from the mentors to scale up the work across BPS. Their proposal and enthusiastic advocacy, along with the many positive anecdotes bubbling up from the schools participating in the pilot project, were enough to convince district leaders, who were already engaged in additional research on the model, to scale up the pilot program across the district.

The district used a two-pronged approach. Some schools were to participate in the full-time release mentoring model, and other schools were to use the existing model of a part-time, school-based mentor (who typically works a full teaching load and mentors part time). District leaders decided that schools with one or two new teachers would participate in the part-time, school-based model, whereas those with three or more new teachers would participate in the full-time release model. This plan made logistical sense in that mentors would not have to travel to a large number of schools, each with only one or two new teachers.

Importantly, principals also had the opportunity to opt out of the full-time program. Although most principals bought in to the full-time model, a handful chose the school-based program (for reasons discussed later). All mentors—full-time and school-based—were required to attend professional development training, and all mentors were renamed new teacher developers (NTDs) to distinguish them from other instructional coaches in the district and the previous mentoring system.

Apart from the bifurcated approach, most other elements of the program were aligned with the NTC model—with one key exception. The program provided support only to teachers in their first year. Schools would be responsible for providing second- and third-year support, and there were no standards or funding to support such efforts. The ratio of mentors to new teachers was 1:14—within the NTC-recommended range—and all mentors (school-based and full-time) were trained by NTC staff using the NTC mentoring curriculum. The only difference was that full-time release mentors received twelve days of professional development training, whereas nonreleased mentors received only six days.

By the third year, collaborative teams of NTC staff and lead BPS NTDs were facilitating the mentor professional development (part of the NTC strategy to build local program capacity). Lead NTDs who served in a co-facilitator role received reduced caseloads to ensure that their new teachers are not shortchanged by the added programmatic duties. New teachers also attend a three-day August Institute for new teachers as well as monthly seminars facilitated by NTDs.

COLLABORATION WITH THE UNION

The Boston Teachers Union (BTU) has a long and solid history of support for BPS teachers. District leaders were aware that any new mentoring program would need to be fully supported by union leadership. When discussion of the new mentoring program first took place, the district and union were already engaged in a legal dispute over issues with the existing program and were also involved in bargaining a new contract. Despite these political sensitivities, both sides determined that the elements of the new mentoring program should be negotiated into the contract. Although the district was the one bringing the program to the negotiating table, the BTU saw this program as an important opportunity to support union goals in two ways: first, it would provide badly needed support to those who needed it most—new teachers; and second, it would provide leadership opportunities for those educators who wanted to advance in the profession but were not interested in becoming administrators.

Both sides recognized that by negotiating the elements of the program and by making the mentoring program part of the bargained contract, they could ensure the program's sustainability despite district leadership changes, school reorganizations, policy shifts, and other factors that often influence reform initiatives. The district and the BTU developed contract language and settled early on the issue of the mentoring program, thus allowing the district to implement it in a timely manner. Once the agreement was reached, the BTU came out in full support of the program, an action that significantly aided efforts to recruit veteran educators to serve as NTDs.

FULL-TIME VERSUS PART-TIME, SCHOOL-BASED MENTORS

Boston Public Schools' decision to use school-based mentors as well as fully released, centrally deployed mentors has provided an opportunity to explore the trade-offs of each strategy. Some research suggests that the fully released mentor has a greater impact on student outcomes.[6] This research confirms much of the sentiment felt across BPS. However, even though many people in the district are avid advocates of full-time mentoring, others believe in part-time, school-based mentoring. These ideological differences reveal key insights into the benefits and drawbacks of each approach.

Ideology 1: Mentors should be full-time and deployed centrally

NTC and BPS program leaders suggest that when mentors are released full time and selected and deployed from a central or district-based office, several benefits accrue.

Mentor selection and capacity to select. District leaders can be trained to use shared criteria (such as a demonstrated mastery of pedagogy and content, a solid understanding of adult learning, an ability to articulate what high-quality teaching looks like, a history of advocacy for new teachers, strong interpersonal skills, etc.) and a common protocol for mentor selection. They are then well informed and well positioned to recruit the most exceptional educators in the system to apply to be mentors. Leaders are also better able to ensure that the mentors selected have reached a common standard of excellence.

On the other hand, few principals receive training in how to develop high-quality mentor programs or how to select effective instructional mentors. Often, they have no shared selection criteria nor a common protocol. Understandably, when asked to identify mentors, many principals choose teachers based on who expresses interest, has corresponding prep times with new teachers, or has the most seniority. Other principals may simply assign teachers to be mentors rather than engage in a selection process at all.[7]

Even more challenging, those schools having the greatest number of beginning teachers are statistically less likely to have a sufficiently large pool of talented veteran teachers to draw on. In hard-to-staff schools, it is common to find that most teachers have less than five years' experience. Teachers in their second or third year of teaching become the mentors to the next class of new teachers. If a mentor program is only as strong as the quality of the mentors, then small and hard-to-staff schools are likely to be at a significant disadvantage in a school-based model.

Sanctioned time. In a full-release, central-deployment model, program leaders can ensure that mentors spend 100 percent of their time focused on mentoring. Because they report to a central office administrator and are not based at only one school site, mentors are less likely to be tapped to take on additional duties that may arise at a site. In school-based programs, however, mentors with release time may be pulled off task to address last-minute school needs, such as covering classes for an absent teacher, making copies for meetings, proctoring exams, and addressing student behavior issues. These additional "duties as assigned" can significantly reduce the amount of time mentors have to work with their new teachers.

In school-based programs where mentors do not have any release time, mentoring interactions must occur before or after school or during common prep times. Mentors may find it almost impossible to observe and collect data on the new teacher's practice—a critical strategy for effective mentoring. Thus, conversations about practice between mentors and beginning teachers take place without data of practice that can highlight critical next steps. In addition, mentors may find it difficult to juggle the needs of their students with the needs of their mentees. Effective teachers (understandably) want to prioritize the needs of their students, thereby neglecting the needs of the beginning teachers they are charged with supporting.

Confidentiality. In the NTC model the relationship between mentors and new teachers is confidential, meaning that the specifics of the interactions are not shared. This practice encourages new teachers to talk openly about their instructional challenges without fear of the information being used against them in their evaluations—or the faculty lounge. Confidentiality helps build trust and rapport, and it supports new teachers in opening up their practice and taking risks that can move their practice forward.

In school-based models where the mentor is supervised by the principal, new teachers sometimes report that it is harder to trust the process. They are aware that mentors report to the principal directly and are fearful that being transparent about the challenges they face may come back to haunt them in future evaluations.

A community of practice for mentors. In a central-deployment model, mentors belong to a community where they receive intensive training, ongoing professional development, and inquiry-based learning about their practice with a cohort of other mentors. In a school-based model, mentors (like teachers) are often isolated in their work and have less access to community building among their mentor peers.

Although Boston provides training for all school-based mentors, many of them report feeling overwhelmed by having to be away from their students for professional development; others report getting push-back from their principals. Program leaders have begun to address the resulting feelings of anxiety and frustration by conducting training during out-of-school hours and spreading it over more days.

Mentor learning curve. Mentors who work all day, every day with beginning teachers are likely to build their skills and knowledge relatively quickly. A full-time mentor with a caseload of fourteen or fifteen teachers is likely to observe, collect data, and collaboratively debrief more than twelve hundred classroom lessons. Such a concentrated focus on teacher performance and its impact on student learning helps mentors become masterful teacher leaders with a well-developed set of skills. In part-time models, where mentors generally work with only one or two teachers and have no community of practice, the learning curve is much steeper—and the progress of skill development much slower.

Ideology 2: Mentors should be part-time and work under a principal

Proponents of the school-based, part-time model argue that the benefits of the school as the central point of services outstrip those of a central-deployment model.

Principal choice in selection and investment in the program. Most principals go to great lengths to select the faculty and staff in their schools. When the central office hires a pool of mentors and deploys them to schools, principals may feel that it undermines their ability to develop an effective team that is aligned with their goals. In a school-based model, principals have control over whom they identify to be the mentor and understand better how the support program fits into their larger vision. The principal, therefore, is likely to have a higher level of investment in the support program and to see the mentor as an important part of the team.

School change. In the central-deployment model, some principals feel that mentors are outside consultants who don't have a sense of the school's ethos or priorities and therefore aren't a part of the school community. This is especially true for those mentors working in a large number of schools (more than four schools at a time).

In a school-based model, it is felt that mentors have deep knowledge of the school's culture and goals and potentially of the relationships that are needed to influence and support school change. Mentors coming from an external source focus on change at the level of the individual teacher, and it is believed that change does not always filter out to support changes at the school level. However, when mentors are assigned to the same school for several years, and particularly if they work with a large number of new teachers at that school, they may have greater influence on school culture.

Informal and on-demand support. Because most of the full-time Boston mentors work in multiple schools, they schedule weekly meetings with new teachers. If a teacher needs extra support, the mentor generally must provide it via phone or e-mail. In contrast, because school-housed mentors are on-site, they are available at all times of the day and can provide informal or in-time support when crises or urgent situations arise.

Integrated support with the school. In schools that provide multilayered support to new teachers, mentoring can take on a new approach. Teachers can get classroom management support from one mentor, instructional guidance from another, planning support from yet another, and content expertise from someone in their department. New teachers benefit from regular collaborative meetings with grade-level and subject-alike teachers that focus on substantive discussion about how to move students forward, providing added layers of support that yield gains in the quality of instructional practice.

In one-on-one mentoring programs that focus on someone who is perceived by some as an external consultant, the integrated layers of support are tangential to the core support. Schools run the risk of thinking that new teachers are "taken care of" and don't seek to provide those integrated support strategies that are powerful in developing teachers.

THE NTC PROGRAM MEETS THE BOSTON TEACHER RESIDENCY PROGRAM

Some observers suggest that the New Teacher Center has the national spotlight on instructionally intensive teacher induction, but others suggest that the Boston Teacher Residency (BTR) program has the national spotlight on new models of teacher preparation. The question might be asked, What happens when these two programs meet?

The BTR was created as an initiative of Boston Public Schools and Boston Plan for Excellence to serve as a "grow your own" strategy. Their mission is to recruit, prepare, and sustain teachers of color and teachers in high-need areas—math, science, special education, and ESL—for the Boston Public Schools. (Historically, there has been a significant gap between the schools' largely Caucasian faculty and the much more diverse student population.) The program seeks to identify and recruit talented potential teachers, especially teachers of color, to earn their teaching credential. Before becoming teachers, residents spend one year in the classroom paired with a high-achieving mentor teacher. Residents are clustered in host schools, in groups of six or more, with an equal number of mentors and a school-based site director. Residents also study at a university to earn their degrees, focusing on coursework that is aligned with the district's priorities. Residents commit to teach in the Boston public schools for a minimum of three years in exchange for tuition reimbursement.

The program was designed for residents to have follow-up support after they graduated. All BTR teachers who wanted to continue receiving support (it is voluntary) were assigned an induction coach for their first three years in the classroom. However, when the decision was made to implement the new NTD mentoring program, program leaders realized that an overlap of resources would be inefficient and possibly confusing for the new teachers. They decided that BTR teachers would receive mentoring support through a district mentor trained through the New Teacher Development Program (the NTC model) in their first year, and support from a BTR induction coach in their second and third years.

The model therefore places residents in Boston classrooms with coteachers or mentors for thirteen months. Then after they receive contracts and begin teaching, they receive an NTDP mentor, and then, in their second and third years, an induction coach hired and trained by the BTR. Some variations on this model have been tried, but this general structure has been implemented for the lion's share of teachers in each cohort.

Although potentially cumbersome, this approach has been executed rather seamlessly and with a great level of success. Program leaders credit the success of this model to, among other things, the close connections between the BTR and NTD programs. This relationship was especially applicable in the early days, as leaders from both programs and from the Office of Human Resources, Office of Teaching and Learning, Office of Instructional Technology, and BPE met to discuss coordination, solve programmatic issues, and discuss the big picture of support for new teachers (an effort supported by the Barr Foundation). Representatives of each of these groups continue to meet monthly.

A key element of these meetings is the review of data (survey results, retention figures, etc.) provided by the external group BPE, the intermediary foundation and research organization supporting reforms in Boston Public Schools. The regular analysis of data provides a reference point for all programs to assess to what extent they are meeting their common goal: ensuring that new teachers receive the support they need to allow them, and their students, to thrive.

BTR and NTD mentors also work closely together to share data about their mentees so that as new teachers transition from one mentor to another, their support can be built from previous efforts. Because neither the BTR nor the NTD mentors are in supervisory roles, they can share data that can help align the work in ways that otherwise might not be viable. This arrangement supports a collaborative team effort to ensure each new teacher's success and provides a seamless approach between preparation and mentoring.

Mentors from both programs also use some of the same frameworks, a practice that helps align messages about instruction. For example, the Dimensions of Effective Teaching—the teaching standards adopted by the district (and that underpin much of the educator and school evaluations)—are fully aligned with the New Teacher Center Professional Teaching Standards/Continuum of Teacher Development and the Boston Teacher Residency Program Core Competencies. The Dimensions standards provide a common language about instruction. As teachers move from their schools of education to their classroom positions, they have already acquired and begun to apply their knowledge of instruction—and coaches from both programs can reinforce and support this learning.

In addition to shared knowledge about instruction, a few policy changes have nurtured the collaborative relationship. One of the key recent decisions was to ensure that all BTR teachers receive a full-time NTD mentor. In the original model, schools that had two or fewer teachers defaulted to having a part-time, school-based NTD. This meant that some BTR teachers would be assigned a part-time NTD based at the school site. The program leaders were aware of the trade-offs of each approach and knew that many of the schools were not doing a sufficient job of compensating for the deficits of the part-time, school-based model. Thus, they requested a change in policy to ensure that BTR teachers always receive a full-time mentor. Such a policy change meant that NTDs would have to take on greater workloads, serve a greater number of schools, and potentially be spread thinner geographically across the districts. In spite of these issues, in the spirit of true collaboration and a sense of shared purpose, NTD program leaders agreed to the change. Each BTR teacher is currently being supported by a full-time NTD.

Also in the spirit of collaboration, there have been coordinated efforts to align BTR coaches and NTDs in the ways they frame their support for teachers. A number of BTR coaches have attended the same training as part-time new teacher developers, and this has allowed them access to many of the same strategies and tools that NTDs are using. Although BTR coaches don't receive the same level of training from NTC as do NTDs, at the very least this alignment allows BTR coaches to understand and reference tools that help new teachers make important connections between support providers. Additionally, each year there are two or three joint full-time NTD/BTR induction coach forums so that the NTDs and the induction coaches can share their experiences and effective strategies in working with the BTR graduates.

Program leaders suggest that even though this level of coordination is a good start, it is limited in scope. They are working on ways to create a much greater level of coordination so that NTDs develop a deeper understanding of the type of training and coursework BTR candidates receive in their pre-service program. Additionally, program leaders report that finding ways to align the various tools and frameworks used in each program would go a long way in helping new teachers navigate the many resources and ideas that are thrown at them.

Is mentoring different for BTR teachers than for others?

With the extensive support received by BTR teachers, one might think they come to the classroom with a slight edge compared with other teachers. NTDs who work with BTR teachers in their first year generally agree that these newbies come to the table with an advantage in three ways.

First, they have a much better sense of the system's culture, understanding the priorities of the system, the available resources, and various initiatives that currently exist. This added knowledge helps them focus on the teaching aspect of their jobs rather than on figuring out their new environment. In contrast, other new teachers are often overwhelmed by information overload in the first year.

Second, BTR teachers generally come with more-realistic expectations of the work. Many new teachers coming in bright-eyed from universities or even some alternative pathway programs tend to have idealized expectations of teaching—both with regard to the relationships they have with their students and the relationships they have with the adults in the school. The abrupt reality check they receive upon starting their jobs—that not all relationships are easy and that teaching is hard—tends to jolt many out of their comfort zone. This difference in expectations is a major contributor to new teacher attrition. BTR teachers tend to come in with more-realistic expectations because they have spent more than a year in the city schools and already have a sense of what it will be like when they have their own classrooms. This experience prepares them mentally and emotionally to quickly focus on the task of educating kids in urban settings.

Third, NTDs also say that BTR teachers tend to be more reflective about their practice and thus more open to support from the NTDs. Although this openness may be an outcome of the factors just described, as well as the intensive training they receive through the program, the result is the same: their work with the mentors tends to be more collaborative and (potentially) more powerful given their receptivity to the support and their desire to improve their practice.

However, NTDs also suggest that the work of understanding and supporting teaching and learning is different for each teacher. In spite of these factors to support their transition, NTDs differentiate support for new BTR teachers in the same way they differentiate support for all new teachers. A few will start strong in some critical teaching areas, others will be strong in other critical teaching areas, and still others will need more support across the board. It is rare that any first-year teacher comes in strong in all critical teaching areas.

Some NTDs also suggest that one of the key factors influencing the competency of the BTR teachers is the quality of the pre-service mentor or coteacher. Many of these coteachers are exemplary teachers and terrific with students, but not all of them are necessarily skilled in working in a mentoring role with a new teacher. The abilities and dispositions of the coteacher can significantly impact the new teacher's experience and, therefore, their instructional development.

Just as mentor selection is the key variable in the New Teacher Development Program (and the NTC model in general), it is also a key element the Boston Teacher Residency program. Mentor selection continues to be a challenge—maybe the most important challenge to overcome—across all programs. BTR is currently exploring opportunities to address this issue, while also seeking to address another key variable in the program's success: identifying and placing residents in schools that have a collaborative culture and desire to support this work.

ONE YEAR OF SUPPORT

Although all BTR teachers, if they so choose, enjoy the support of a mentor or induction coach for the first three years they are in the classroom, new teachers coming from other pathways receive only one year of support. People in many layers of the system are beginning to feel the repercussions of not having a second or third year of support integrated into the program. District leaders, mentors, and new teachers themselves seem to agree that the program is great, but it needs to be extended.

One NTD said that she was "worried about letting go of these teachers after year one, when they've just started figuring out what to do . . . it's the follow-up years that are going to be what matters most—how they apply what they've learned." A district leader noted, "If we had the funds available, we'd absolutely make sure teachers got a mentor for more than one year. But we don't even have the funding right now to make sure all first-year teachers get access to a full-time mentor." One teacher summed up his feelings by stating, "I just didn't know what I didn't know in the first year. I mean, it was my second year before I started figuring it out—before I started getting a handle on the right questions to ask."

The hope has been that school leaders will take on the important work of supporting new teachers in their second and third years through more intensive support. However, no structure, guidelines, or funding yet exists to support more-robust mentoring of these teachers. This has resulted in a slide back to school-based, traditional contexts. Where principals are committed to nurturing learning communities and identifying creative structures to allow for one-on-one mentoring, new teachers are thriving. Where principals cannot provide support for second- and third-year teachers, there is a question as to how much potential is being lost. Some observers have questioned the impact a program can have if it serves teachers only in the first year, when they are, as one principal put it, "in survival mode—before they develop enough experience to do what they need to do, to get the kids where they need to go."

OUTREACH TO PRINCIPALS

Program leaders took a multipronged approach to reaching out to principals. One of the most successful strategies has been to provide choices along with structure. For example, from the beginning, principals could opt out of the program if they ideologically opposed the full-time model. In the first phases of matching NTDs with schools, program leaders also gave principals bios of the mentors they were considering assigning and asked principals to select from the list. Although many principals ultimately agreed with the program leadership's recommendations, the act of giving them the choice went a long way in helping school leaders feel included in the process—and likely fostered greater feelings that the mentors were a part of the school team.

A second strategy was to provide principals with information they could use themselves in supporting new teachers. Rather than focus solely on the mentoring program, mentors and program leaders disseminated a toolkit and provided training with specific guidelines on policies and practices that would help new teachers succeed. For example, principals received information on "what your new teachers want to know," "best practices on inducting your new teachers into your school," and agenda templates for effective school-based induction days.

Program leaders say that they are still trying to gain traction on the issue of supporting school leaders to create the conditions that lead to success for new teachers. They are trying creative approaches in administrative breakfasts, and building the capacity of the mentors to talk with principals about key conditions, such as new teacher assignments, professional learning communities, teaming new teachers with other networks of support, and focusing in on strong instructional support strategies.

Many of these strategies are well received by principals, especially when good relationships have been established between the administrator and the mentor. However, when the relationships are more strained, it is appreciably more difficult to broach issues of working conditions, especially because NTDs are often seen as being on the same "line" as other teachers. One NTD says, "I think it's great that I'm a union member along with the [new teachers], and I have no supervisory or evaluative authority. I like that. At the same time, it means that the only leverage . . . I have to support [principals] to move forward, when I advocate for the new teacher, is the leverage they grant me through our relationship."

Some observers suggest that the relationships typically are framed by the management style of the principal; the more top-down the approach, the less the administrator is interested in having collaborative discussions that may lead to better policies for new teachers. Some mentors suggest that it is particularly hard to approach such conversations in "toxic" school environments that do not value or support the voice of the teacher.

A key piece of the outreach strategy to principals is also focused on the confidentiality agreements, historically a sticking point for some principals, who want full access to information about their own teachers. To address this concern, program leaders invited principals who had already bought in to the idea of confidentiality to speak with other principals and provide additional testimonials. This was a powerful strategy that seemed to resonate with many school leaders.

Program leaders admit that it has taken time for principals to fully buy in and, even then, buy-in depends highly on the relationship between the mentor and the school leader. There continues to be some resistance to confidentiality, because some school leaders feel they could do a more powerful job of supporting their new teachers instructionally if they could reinforce (and be reinforced by) what the mentor is doing in the classroom.

TEACHER NETWORKS AND CROSS-SCHOOL INTERVISITATIONS

Every month, new teachers participate in seminars to deepen their learning about instruction. These seminars are always aligned with the work that NTDs are focusing on and are grounded in the teaching standards adopted by the district (Dimensions of Effective Teaching). As a part of the seminar series, program leaders have developed a cross-school intervisitation program. In this program, groups of new teachers visit schools in the district and observe educators handpicked by program leaders. Afterward, with the NTD who was leading the visit, they debrief what they saw and discuss how they might apply it to their own teaching practice.

This protocol builds on research that says new teachers who are engaged in networks with teachers outside their own school tend to remain in schools longer. It also supports a primary goal of the program, which is to open up the practice of teaching and learning so that educators (new and experienced) can learn from one another and foster instructional progress within a professional, supportive environment.

The intervisitations have been successful for the most part, but there has been resistance from school leaders who are not enthusiastic about having their new teachers leave their buildings to observe classrooms in other schools. Mentors occasionally try to set up in-school visitations, but time, schedules, and coordination problems often inhibit frequent sessions.

Program leaders hope to raise the emphasis on in-school visitations in future years.

OUTCOMES

District leaders report that after the first year of implementation, retention rates increased to approximately 80 percent, up from approximately 71 percent. Moreover, a specific goal of Boston Public Schools is to recruit and retain more teachers of color. Retention rates for first-year teachers of color have improved significantly, rising from 73 percent in 2005–2006 to 83 percent in 2006–2007.

However, district leaders also assert that the increase in retention cannot be connected directly to the mentoring program alone, because a number of policies were changed during the time of implementation. For example, the overhaul of human resources to support new teachers was beginning to get traction in these years. The retention rates have remained steady since the implementation of the program.

LESSONS LEARNED

Boston's New Teacher Development program provides a laboratory setting to explore questions that have perplexed the field. It allows us to better understand such critical issues as the trade-offs between part-time and full-time mentoring, ways to effectively build bridges with school leaders, and ways to create sustainability of a program at scale. The following section provides some thoughts and reflections on these topics, yielding successful strategies, challenges, and key questions for leaders seeking to build or support their own programs.

Union contract as a lever for sustainability

The district's decision to partner with the teachers union was a critical part of developing credibility among teachers and gaining support for implementing the model with fidelity. The program is a win-win for both parties, because it supports traditional union values (such as improved working conditions for new teachers and leadership opportunities for veteran teachers) while also addressing district goals of closing the student achievement gap and improving instruction throughout the system.

Both the union and the district also saw the union contract as a means of making the program sustainable. As leadership and policy changes continue to pervade education over time, district leaders might consider the bargaining agreement as a consistent and binding force that can ride out the tides of change.

Full-time versus part-time mentoring

The full-time mentoring program enjoys strong and deep support throughout Boston Public Schools. Yet some stakeholders within the system (and some in other systems) are ideologically more aligned with the idea of part-time, school-based mentoring in which mentors operate under the supervision of the principal.

Although the NTC model focuses on full-time, centrally deployed mentors, there are many benefits to a part-time model that supports new teacher development. The argument should not be about which approach is better. Rather, because both approaches have benefits and drawbacks, the question is, How does one compensate for the gaps that exist in each model?

For example, consider a full-time model in which a mentor comes in once or twice a week to provide support. Often that mentor cannot be there right away if an emergency pops up. Programs can address this gap by working with principals to provide a school-based buddy mentor, in addition to the full-time district mentor, so that the new teacher has support to fall back on if last-minute issues arise. Similarly, in a part-time model, the primary gap is a lack of sanctioned time for mentors to meet with new teachers (and time to observe their new teachers' practice). Programs can develop creative schedules and provide partial release time to ensure that new teachers receive the recommended hours of interaction. Programs can also enable mentors to attend training regularly and visit new teachers' classrooms to see and collect data on their practice. If some release time is provided, it is critical that school leaders commit to not assigning other duties so that mentors are not pulled off-task.

One study compared the district's full-time model to the school-based, part-time model, finding that the full-time model had stronger outcomes in teacher practice and student achievement. However, the study also showed that some of the anticipated gaps that exist in the part-time model were indeed present in the district's program (for example, part-time mentors observed new teacher classrooms less than did full-time mentors).

If districts are serious about making school-based, part-time models effective, a number of intensive initiatives will be needed to guard against the strong tendency to revert to traditional, ineffective mentoring.

Multiple strategies for reaching out to principals

The multipronged approach to reaching out to principals was effective. Providing a few mentors to choose from was a good way to give principals agency, and it supported principals' view of mentors as part of the school team. Having other principals speak in favor of confidentiality also was viewed as successful. Toolkits and other informational support to help administrators better understand and support new teachers were also well received.

Efforts by NTDs to support principals in transforming working conditions seemed to be more challenging. Where relationships with principals were strong, new teacher advocacy was easier, but in the areas where new teachers needed the most advocacy—in toxic school environments—it seemed harder. Training for mentors in providing effective advocacy in these settings might serve to support such efforts in the future. Districts might also consider other avenues of support for school leaders to help create the types of environments that will let all teachers thrive.

Linking preparation with mentoring

Historically, coordination with schools of education regarding mentoring has been inadequate, and coordination with the universities around Boston may still leave something to be desired. But the partnership of the Boston Teacher Residency Program and the New Teacher Development Program has proven that aligned support is possible.

Critical factors in this alignment include long-term, consistent relationship building throughout the process. Because the groups meet regularly (along with other district stakeholders) and the leaders are in constant communication, the level of coordination is ongoing. It has been extremely helpful to have data (especially from an external source, such as the Boston Plan for Excellence) to use as a reference point for ways the programs can improve coordination on the ground. Additionally, the efforts between BTR coaches and NTD mentors to share and build on data regarding each new teacher have helped create a seamless transition of support as new teachers move through each of the programs.

Through ongoing relationship building, leaders from both programs have established a sense of trust and common purpose. This rapport has helped both programs avoid the turf wars that sometimes damage district reform efforts. In addition, it has meant that policy changes to support one another's efforts can be prioritized even when they have some negative repercussions for one of the programs.

This level of coordination and deep collaboration, although ideal, is far from typical. NTC encourages districts to identify opportunities for coordination with surrounding universities and alternative certification programs. This is a challenge for cities that work with large numbers of universities and programs. In the BPS case, the district works with only one program—the BTR program—and that potentially eases coordination.

Facilitating intervisitations

The intervisitation component of Boston's NTD program supports new teachers in observing, collecting data on, and debriefing the practice of teachers in other schools. This activity gives new teachers rich opportunities for networking with other teachers (new and experienced) outside their own context. Intervisitation furthers new teachers' understanding of teaching practices and helps them draw out the nuances of good teaching practice, regardless of school context. It also helps move systems away from the traditional model of teaching in isolation and supports the wide-scale opening of instructional practice for ongoing collaborative learning.

Because systems generally are not yet open to this new paradigm, principals may be nervous about allowing teachers out of their buildings. District leaders can support this transition by communicating about the goals and hopes for this type of approach throughout the system. Additionally, mentors can strengthen relationships with principals and enhance new teacher learning by working with school leaders to identify and facilitate more intervisitations with other teachers in the school community.

Multiple years of support

When asked to identify the biggest challenge of the program, the most consistent response, from district leaders to teachers, was that the program ended after one year. The caliber of mentors is perceived as strong, but if they are providing support only during new teachers' "survival" year, it will not be as deep or powerful as if the support continued into the second and third years, when teachers are just figuring out the "right questions to ask."

District leaders might consider a model similar to the BTR program, where only second- and third-year teachers who request an induction coach or mentor receive one. Additionally, the district might consider tapping in to the strong foundation community to support additional years of support, because foundations have been critical players in taking the program to the point it is today.

6

New York City
Department of Education

Students have the best chance of reaching their potential when their classrooms
are led by exceptional educators. We've worked hard to bring the best and brightest teachers to New York City's public schools, and we are committed to providing
them with the training, guidance, and support they need to be successful from the
first day they enter the classroom.

—Joel Klein, chancellor, New York City Department of Education

BACKGROUND AND PROGRAM DESIGN

In the summer of 2003, the New York City Department of Education
(DOE) invited organizations to help extend and deepen the city's existing mentoring model—a collaborative effort between the DOE and the
Teachers Center, a division of the United Federation of Teachers (UFT).
The DOE was concerned about high rates of attrition of new teachers. In
addition, the costs related to attrition were draining the human resources
budget, with potentially millions of dollars lost each year in recruitment
costs alone. At the same time, research was emerging showing the significant negative impact of persistent teacher turnover, often on the most vulnerable students. (See box, "State Policy Context.")

Leaders in the Human Resources office were determined to transform
the way they inducted new teachers into the system. In late 2003, they

---

State Policy Context

In 2004, the New York Board of Regents modified the teacher certification requirement, mandating that all new teachers having less than one year's teaching experience in New York receive a high-quality mentoring experience in their first year of teaching. Although the regulation was unfunded, it provided guidelines that emphasized the need to move away from historical buddy systems to new programs using best practices in mentoring. Additionally, the state legislature has appropriated funds to support the development and implementation of mentor teacher internship programs in local school districts and for instructional programs at boards of cooperative educational services (BOCES). Funding for this program is subject to yearly approval by the legislature.

---

reached out to the New Teacher Center to implement the largest mentoring reform initiative in the country, a $36 million investment. The systemwide initiative contained many of the components of the NTC model, including a systematic mentor-selection process focused on the qualities of effective mentors, extensive ongoing professional development and communities of practice for mentors, use of formative assessments based on teacher and student data, integration of professional teaching standards, full release time for mentors, and partnership with the teachers union. The NTC provided training for mentors through mentor academies (four times a year) and mentor forums (twice a month) and partnered with the DOE to provide ongoing consultation and support for implementation.

The New York City initiative did not include three elements of the NTC induction model. First, the program supported only first-year teachers (whereas the NTC model calls for at least two years of support for new teachers). Second, the ratio of new teachers to full-time release mentors was 17:1, as opposed to the recommended maximum ratio suggested by NTC of 15:1 (and even lower in hard-to-staff settings). The ratio grew beyond 17:1 in many cases after implementation challenges arose. Third, New York City struggled to create a successful systemwide structure for engaging principals in meaningful ways to support the program.

Regional directors were hired in each of the eleven main regional offices in the city to oversee all aspects of the program, including hiring, matching, and supervision of mentors and developing a collaborative community of practice for mentors. To lead the program and support mentor development in each of the regions, each regional director was paired with a UFT mentor liaison (an instructional and professional development leader affiliated with the UFT Teachers Center and selected by the teachers union). At its peak, the program released approximately four hundred mentors full time to support the approximately six thousand new teachers coming into the system.

ISSUES AND OPPORTUNITIES IN THE NEW YORK MODEL

Any education reform effort seeking to create change at such a large scale (1.2 million children) is sure to encounter challenges during implementation, and the New York initiative was no different. Year 1 challenges included antiquated data systems that were not set up to locate or track new teachers, unforeseen loopholes in the mentor-selection process, support strategies that conflicted with other initiatives, difficulty in engaging principals, and internal disconnects between the Human Resources Department and the Teaching and Learning Department regarding the goals of the program.[1] Although these issues may be more pronounced in large urban districts, NTC finds that programs undergo a unique programmatic learning curve and that it often takes time to iron out implementation wrinkles.

By the second and third years of the program, however, the city began to see the seeds it planted grow and saw promising signs of success in all the components it had included in the program design. School officials had developed a sophisticated selection process that incorporated teams of experienced instructional leaders, rigorous interviews (including role plays and situational problem solving, and use of videotapes to assess the candidate's eye for and approach toward targeted instructional interventions).

In addition, there was evidence that new teachers and mentors were becoming active users of student and teacher data to drive instructional progress. In a survey that went out to all six thousand new teachers (with a response rate of more 75 percent), approximately 80 percent of new teachers reported that mentors were collecting and using data to inform conversations about their practice and that their mentors were being helpful or extremely helpful in developing their confidence, skills, and knowledge in teaching.

This use of formative data to drive instructional change represented a huge cultural shift in how educators viewed and approached their support efforts. Instead of focusing on personal opinion or imposing their own expert knowledge of teaching on new teachers, mentors across the board were beginning to understand how to collect and use evidence of new teacher practice and provide real-time feedback to teachers in ways that would improve instruction. This cultural shift happened to align well with the data-driven focus the system was taking in other major city initiatives.

Data issues

Although the use of formative data was promising, a number of obstacles impeded understanding of the full impact of the program on teacher and student outcomes. The challenges in collecting and analyzing data at a central level were significant for a number of reasons. For example, it wasn't clear which teachers were eligible for mentoring, because different layers of the system had different interpretations of the term "new teacher." Moreover, in many cases internal and state databases had challenges in talking to one another when analysts sought to triangulate information. Gaps existed between resignation reporting and central processing time, an issue common to most large urban districts.

There was also some internal confusion within the district as to the reliability of information coming out about the program. One report from the Human Resources Department said that attrition of new teachers who were mentored was 7 percent, compared with a 12 percent rate for new teachers who were not mentored, and it asserted that the program was helping cut attrition rates by almost half. This report did not go fully public, however, because there were questions about the soundness of the data. The city decided to partner with an external independent researcher to identify the impact of the program.

Research outcomes

An independent study by a researcher at Columbia Business School provided promising findings and sobering truths.

I find strong relationships between measures of mentoring quality and teachers' claims regarding the impact of mentors on their success in the classroom, but weaker evidence of effects on teacher absences, retention, and student achievement. The most consistent finding is that retention within a particular school is higher when a mentor has previous experience working in that school, suggesting that an important part of mentoring may be the provision of school specific knowledge. I also find evidence that student achievement in both reading and math were higher among teachers that received more hours of mentoring, supporting the notion that time spent working with a mentor does improve teaching skills.[2]

This report reinforces for the NTC two critical findings. First, time for mentoring is paramount in supporting new teacher practice. Second, the mentors' knowledge of their new teachers' schools and engagement in the school community are critical to success.

The promising news is that new teachers who receive a minimum threshold of time with their mentors (approximately forty-five hours per year in NYC, or one hour per week) show more positive student achievement gains as a result of the work with the mentor compared with those who spent thirty-five hours per year with their mentors. Specifically, "an additional ten hours of mentoring [can be] expected to raise student achievement by 0.05 standard deviations in math and 0.04 standard deviations in reading."[3] These gains reinforce the program's fundamental conceptual framework. When new teachers are supported by well-selected, highly trained mentors and are given time to engage in classroom-based instructional interventions, new teachers will improve their practice sooner, and the students of those teachers (often the most underserved and highest-need students) will have better outcomes and more opportunities to succeed.

The more sobering part of the data, however, is that most teachers in New York City received less than the number of hours recommended by the NTC for mentoring interactions. (NTC recommends 1.5–2.5 hours of support per week.) Consequently, student achievement gains were not felt widely across the city.

Time with mentors

Why was there diminished time for many of the new teachers in the system? There were two compounding factors: the ratio of mentors to beginning teachers, and the number of schools assigned to mentors.

Ratios of mentors to beginning teachers. The ratio of new teachers to mentors was 17:1, greater than the recommended 15:1 maximum. In some cases, this ratio ballooned to overwhelming ratios as high as 21:1. Many teachers thus received significantly decreased support, because it was physically impossible for mentors to meet the time allocations for all the teachers in their portfolios. In some cases, mentors gave some teachers more support than others, perhaps based on receptivity, the need for support, or other factors. In other cases, mentors trimmed the amount of time across the board for all their new teachers. Either way, the result was significantly diminished time for a large subset of new teachers.

Number of schools assigned to mentors. Some regions prioritized content matches at the secondary level, ensuring that mentors had expertise in the same subject areas as their new teachers wherever possible. This decision was based on research that documents the importance of emphasizing content knowledge in the preparation and support of teachers. The higher the number of content matches, the more schools a mentor must work in to allow the matching.

For example, a mentor with a background in math might be matched with only one or two teachers in a given school, thus increasing the number of schools in which the mentor supported teachers. With the subject-matter matching approach, some New York City mentors were visiting teachers in more than six or seven—even ten—schools. When travel time and time for finding parking were accounted for (not an insignificant amount of time in the city), along with the scheduling challenges that arose from being spread too thin, mentors found the amount of time they had for interactions with new teachers significantly diminished.

Both factors together meant that most of the new teachers in New York City schools received no more than forty-five minutes of support—about half the recommended time.

Knowledge of school culture

The other finding from the independent study also provided learning for the NTC. Beginning teachers supported by mentors who had previous experience working in the new teacher's school (either as a teacher or a mentor) showed increased retention rates compared with those supported by mentors who had no prior experience in the school. The study corroborates what NTC leaders have learned through experience: mentoring interactions become more meaningful when mentors have a solid understanding of the school culture. Moreover, when mentors can explicate connections between, on the one hand, individualized instructional support strategies for the new teacher they support and, on the other hand, collective instructional initiatives at the school level, the support is more aligned. Furthermore, as evidenced by this recent study, the support is more effective.

THE TRANSITION TO LOCAL CONTROL

The chancellor of the New York City schools during implementation of this program was Joel Klein, who was hired by Mayor Michael Bloomberg to transform the city's school system after the mayor was given local control over the school system. The first few years of this administration were spent trying to bring quality and consistency to New York City schools. Klein, in collaboration with Mayor Bloomberg's office, worked to achieve this goal by consolidating control of the schools and making nearly all operational and instructional decisions through a central office in downtown Manhattan. A number of centralized programs focusing on support for schools to improve student outcomes emerged through this process. One of them was the comprehensive mentoring program.

Once the department determined that the effort was successful and the system's capacity had been increased, it chose to transition to a decentralized system of control. This decision emerged as Chancellor Klein determined that each school—and more importantly, its principal—now needed full autonomy to realize each school's potential. One city official refers to the paradigm shift as a lab environment where central offices served as "an incubator for promising ideas—promoting understanding and development of best practices," and then once ideas were fully developed, "pushing the ideas out to the schools." The schools were then responsible for carrying the ideas to fruition and innovating wherever possible.

For principals to help launch New York schools into the next phase of success, the power structure of school decision making and programming had to be shifted from centralized control to the schools. In exchange for greater accountability (and high-stakes consequences for failing schools), principals were empowered to make nearly all decisions related to hiring, management, programming, ways that teachers were supported, and, most importantly, budget. To make this type of approach useful for principals, the central office had to significantly augment school budgets. It was therefore politically and logistically critical to devolve funding from virtually all centralized programs to the schools. Schools could purchase programs on their own but would no longer receive substantive instructional support from the central office. Because the mentoring program clearly fell into the category of a centralized, instruction-based program, it was one of the programs devolved to the school level.

The central Office of New Teacher Induction made initial efforts to reach out to schools to maintain the full-time mentoring program within this new organization. However, a major obstacle emerged: general fund resources were devolved to the schools without a specific earmark for a mentoring program. In addition, the funds were allocated to schools using a formula that was not based on the anticipated number of new teachers. As a result, schools with large numbers of new teachers in the fall would not have received a concomitant bump in funding to support more mentoring.

Although all principals received a lump sum for their budget that included funds for mentoring, the explicit lack of earmarking made it difficult for some principals to understand. One principal exclaimed, "I was really upset when I learned mentoring would be coming out of our budgets—that they hadn't set aside funding for the mentors. I don't have a big budget. It's like, I could have a mentor or [an assistant principal]. And I couldn't have both." In the new model of local control, comprehensive full-time mentoring for new teachers was often not a priority in schools with limited budgets.

An additional challenge was that schools were clustered into networks of twenty to twenty-five schools that were not geographically based. Schools could pool resources and collaborate across the network to share the services of a full-time mentor or mentors, but short timelines made it difficult. This option was further complicated by the fact that network-based, fully released mentors might end up being deployed in schools located across all five boroughs—a logistical nightmare.

Naturally, as principals sought to prioritize their school budgets, there were many competing demands. Intensive instructional mentoring by a fully released mentor was an expensive item given that few schools would have fifteen new teachers (considered a full mentor caseload). This was exacerbated by the fact that many principals felt that they could better support their new teachers with school-based mentors and professional development aligned with the rest of the school's instructional approach. In addition, a number of schools were interested in hiring as many experienced teachers as possible. Although these teachers would be more expensive, many principals felt a more veteran staff would be more beneficial for kids.

Unfortunately, most principals had not been provided sufficient information about the critical principles and benefits of comprehensive induction programs. Despite persistent efforts by program leaders and mentors, a number of obstacles thwarted principals' understanding of the critical work that the mentors in their schools had been doing with their new teachers.[4] Now, without a specific allocation of funds for mentoring, most principals opted to use the funds for general budget purposes, devoting to mentoring only enough funds to meet state requirements.

However, not all principals have taken this action. A number of principals—those who were educated about the needs of new teachers, as well as those who were already on board—are determined to create schools that have robust structures to support new teacher effectiveness. Some of these programs employ full-time mentors, team-based, collaborative mentoring, coteaching with structured protocols, or other models that incorporate many of the NTC's principles of high-quality mentoring and induction (see chapter 3).

The devolution of the mentoring program has highlighted a continuum of principal knowledge. Principals who understand the importance of high-quality mentoring have put resources into selecting exceptional staff to serve as mentors, releasing them to work significant amounts of time with new teachers, providing training for mentors, and integrating multifaceted support strategies. On the other hand, principals who did not have access to information on the specific needs of new teachers or the differences between high-quality mentoring and buddy systems have ended up implementing more traditional forms of mentoring. In these cases, the process for selecting mentors is haphazard (e.g., focusing on who is available rather than who might be most qualified), there is little or no training for mentors, and there is limited, if any, release time to allow the mentor to observe and discuss teacher practice. Most of the schools fall somewhere between the two ends of this continuum.

The New York City DOE recognized the importance of supporting principals and schools in creating strong approaches to teacher development, including teacher mentoring. As a result, DOE officials implemented a number of strategies focused on human capital development that also build support for mentoring of early career teachers.

Establishing an office of teacher development

In an effort to shift more schools in the direction of higher-quality mentoring without issuing mandates that require them to do so (and thus disempowering principals), the central office created a new division, the Office of Teacher Development. It used this opportunity to bring together a number of programs and initiatives that focus on teacher learning and effectiveness, including teacher induction, partnerships with pre-service institutions, teacher evaluation, support for teachers in their first few years, and so on. Part of this effort also involves a heightened interest in learning how to collect data on and assess teacher effectiveness.

Strategic site-based mentor plans

All schools are required to develop strategic plans that explain exactly how they will support mentoring for new teachers. These plans are developed with support from central or network staff, and schools are allowed great flexibility in how programs are designed. Best practices are encouraged but not mandated. For example, the department developed and disseminated two publications: *Principal's Guide to School-Based Mentoring* and *The Principal's Early Planning Guide for Mentoring.* All schools are required to show in the plan how they will meet state regulations for mentoring for all first-year teachers as well as general compliance criteria.

Lead instructional mentors (LIMs)

Recognizing that the city had invested in and developed mentors over the three years of the full-release program and that these mentors were skilled resources for improving teacher effectiveness, the DOE designed a program that would build upon mentors' knowledge and skills. The Office of Teacher Development hired approximately seventy former mentors to serve as lead instructional mentors (LIMs), with the primary task of providing professional development to site-based mentors and coaches who would be supporting new teachers. LIMs work with twenty to thirty schools and differentiate their support based on schools' specific needs (such as professional development for staff on teaching standards, one-on-one training for mentors, and general compliance support) in much the same way that they previously tailored their assistance for new teachers.

As LIMs work with schools, they must find ways to integrate their efforts with those of the network staff—teams of support personnel dedicated to working with one specific network of schools. Whereas the LIMs' expertise and experience focus on advancing an individual teacher's ability to improve student learning, the network-based support personnel focus on school-level change. LIMs worked for three years to develop skills in accelerating the practice of new teachers in one-on-one settings, using individualized coaching strategies and focusing on classroom- and student-level data specific to that teacher. The network support staff, in many instances, are trained to look at schoolwide practices, such as professional development for all teachers, common areas for improvement in various classroom contexts, school accountability protocols, innovative scheduling solutions, and the like. The two skill sets, although complementary, are not yet integrated or aligned.

One network team staff person in the first year of this program commented, "We've gotten training in the professional teaching standards. And [the LIMs have] received training in the accountability tools. But still, there just seems to be a lack of coherence between our efforts." Another LIM noted, "Our areas of expertise are different . . . and we just haven't figured out where they intersect yet."

Professional teaching standards and the NTC continuum

One strategy that helps align school improvement efforts with the efforts to develop each individual teacher's effectiveness is the use of professional teaching standards in both mentoring and school accountability measures. The LIMs were extensively trained as instructional mentors to use professional teaching standards and the NTC Continuum of Teacher Development as important tools to guide their mentoring, frame their interactions with beginning teachers, and formatively assess a new teacher's developing practice. Not only were these tools central features of the mentors' work, but also more than eighteen thousand beginning teachers were at various stages of using these tools to guide their own growth and practice.

Recently, these two documents were introduced into the process of school accountability. In doing so, New York has attempted to create a bridge that spans the work of these two historically disconnected endeavors: school-level and teacher-level change. Now, using this common framework for looking at and assessing instruction allows principals, assistant principals, LIMs, leadership teams, site-based mentors, network leaders, and all other school staff focused on supporting instructional improvement to be on the same page as they talk about instruction and instructional improvement.

As a part of the effort to bridge this disconnect, the professional teaching standards and NTC Continuum of Teacher Development were integrated into the new school review process, a central component of a principal's evaluation that shifted attention to the use of professional teaching standards almost overnight. "I think when principals had to look at the Continuum, really look at it, that's when we started getting the entry points we needed to work with schools more meaningfully," offers one LIM. Principals and school leadership teams see the value of having a common framework that can guide their analysis of instruction and are seeking to use the tool to assess instruction in all of their classrooms. One principal says, "It's giving us a language to talk about instruction. It makes me wonder how we've gone so long without having a language."

Given their knowledge and experience using the Continuum and professional teaching standards, the LIMs are, of course, the ones best able to provide professional development using these tools. They help school leaders understand how to use the documents as something more than an accountability tool. LIMs support school leaders in using the document to collaboratively assess new teacher needs, determine opportunities to address those needs, and identify goals that will support a teacher's instructional growth over time. Recent NTC analyses suggest that schools are finding new opportunities to build on and use the teaching standards in ways that support collaborative professional communities of practice, coaching and mentoring, and other strategies that lead to improved teaching and learning throughout schools.

Training for university field staff supporting alternatively certified teachers

The Office of Teacher Recruitment and Quality has been engaged in an additional effort with the New Teacher Center to develop and train more than 150 university field staff. These people—serving as clinical faculty, supervisors, and mentors—support the approximately three thousand new teachers who have gone through an alternative certification process known as the Teaching Fellows Program, a collaboration of the New York City Department of Education and The New Teacher Project (not to be confused with the New Teacher Center, based in Santa Cruz). In collaboration with several stakeholders working with the New York City Department of Education, the NTC has developed a rubric modified from the NTC Continuum of Teacher Development.

This new tool, called the Fellow Development Index (FDI), was developed through an extensive effort to ask instructional leaders throughout the system to identify those elements of the Continuum that they believed met two criteria: (1) the elements they believed to have greatest impact on student achievement and (2) the elements that are most observable during occasional drop-in visits. The NTC, in partnership with the district, then created a one-page front-to-back rubric focusing on these elements, to be used as an observation tool to assess teacher skill.

University field staff, who typically visit their new teachers in the classroom about once a month, record classroom evidence during their observations and then use the data to assess where the new teachers' practice might fall on this FDI rubric.

The field staff and program leaders use the assessments at an aggregate level only to look at trends that may impact recruitment and training methods. (The information is not used to evaluate individual teachers.) Department and NTC leaders have been pleased to learn that the ratings on the rubric are consistent with administrator reports of teachers, along with teacher self-reports and student value-added data.

The NTC also works with the field staff to support their development in using the data collected, along with other formative assessment data, to improve individualized support for the new teachers.

LESSONS LEARNED AND IMPLICATIONS

Time spent working with a given new teacher is a critical element of effective mentoring. Independent researchers find that new teachers who spent more time with their mentors had better student outcomes than those who spent less time with their mentors. Yet in the implementation of New York City's comprehensive mentoring program, most new teachers had less than the optimum amount of time with their mentors. This may have been the result of the high teacher-to-mentor ratios or the high number of schools that mentors served.

NTC continues to underscore the need to cap mentor-to-teacher ratios at 1:15 and strongly recommends that mentors serve no more than four schools in a given year. By lowering school ratios, programs can also improve mentors' knowledge of the school culture and populations, something that is important for improving retention, according to a recent report.[5]

Professional teaching standards, school change, and teacher development

The New York City case study describes a unique and potentially powerful approach to building a systemwide platform for teacher development by using professional teaching standards in concert with the NTC Continuum of Teacher Development. By using these documents across the system and integrating them into the school accountability process, New York City helps connect two historically different entry points for educational improvement. One approach traditionally targets schools as the unit of change, focusing on schoolwide practices, school-level data, and instructional initiatives that can be generalized to the entire teacher population. In the other, the teacher is considered the unit of change, and efforts focus on addressing the individual needs of each teacher (especially new teachers) through one-on-one coaching, the use of classroom- and teacher-specific data, and individual interventions.

The two approaches to change should be interwoven, but creating structures to support such an alignment can be challenging. The rollout of the teaching standards as part of the new school evaluation structure is an attempt to bridge this disconnect as school leaders, network staff, site-based mentors, and LIMs figure out how to incorporate a common framework for understanding and assessing instruction into their daily routines. As a result, the Continuum, professional teaching standards, and other formative assessment tools are being used with teachers in one-on-one coaching conversations, in collaborative team conversations (e.g., grade- and discipline-level meetings), in professional development days for all school staff, and in goal-setting conversations between school leaders and new teachers.

These efforts suggest important lessons for the field, supporting more exploration into strategies that foster a sharing of teaching standards throughout school communities without loss of a focus on individualized mentoring support for new teachers.

Engaging principals

During New York City's devolution of power from the central office to schools, NTC became aware of the persistent gap in communication about the features of high-quality mentoring and the benefits that the system could realize when such a program is implemented well. Principals may be the first to prioritize such programs when they understand how significant the gains could be if they are successful in making the least-effective teachers in their school among the most-effective teachers, but in the New York case the information was not packaged in ways that seemed relevant or pressing for many school leaders. Even where there was interest, it seemed that many principals did not have easily accessible information to help them figure out how to ensure that best practices of mentoring fit into their own school context.

The NTC has recently launched new initiatives to help articulate and advocate for mentoring, specifically for school leaders, who are often overwhelmed with information overload and competing priorities. NTC also encourages districts to develop programs to create messages tailored to this audience and thereby improve engagement with this critical constituency.

Targeted funding for mentoring

Having program-specific funding for mentoring communicates across the system that new teacher retention and effectiveness are priorities. If school systems do not protect these funds, then principals, and others charged with teacher mentoring, will not be able to support rigorous programs when confronted by myriad competing demands.

But protected funds are not enough. In systems where principals have the primary responsibility, funding must be accompanied by information about the benefits and essential elements of quality programs. This information is not typically common knowledge and is often counterintuitive for principals who are thinking about implementing staffing plans, managing competing instructional initiatives, and complying with central office, as well as local, expectations and demands.

Multi-faceted approach

New York City has transitioned to local control over a centralized, comprehensive approach, and the district continues to implement a number of strategies for supporting new teachers. These efforts include partnerships with schools of education and alternative certification programs, a modified train-the-trainers program that builds on the knowledge of former mentors, and the rollout of teaching standards and other formative assessment tools. The DOE's multifaceted approach indicates a desire to create an aligned system of support for teacher development and accountability.

One of the challenges faced by New York City's current structure is figuring out how to help all principals see that the work of individualized support for teachers is core to the work of transforming schools. Strong instructional mentoring of new teachers—using a system that is aligned with the principles of high-quality induction—is a critical factor in that transformative work. District leaders are hopeful that their sustained efforts to empower and support administrators across the city, along with their push to build a strong vision for high-quality instruction, will yield in robust supports for new, and all teachers, and ultimately, better outcomes for kids.

7

Chicago Public Schools

If we are going to move our system forward, we have to make sure that our teach-ers have the opportunity to achieve their best. That's why we are making new teachers a priority . . . because they deserve the opportunity to succeed.

—Barbara Eason-Watkins, chief education officer,
Chicago Public Schools

BACKGROUND AND PROGRAM DESIGN

The Chicago mentoring program represents a new model for NTC in two ways. First, rather than the district overseeing most aspects of the imple-mentation of the program (as is typical in most of our partnerships), the NTC opened a Chicago-based office, called the Chicago New Teacher Center. Full-time NTC employees were hired and charged with imple-menting most aspects of the program: the selection and hiring of staff, all mentor training, new teacher professional development, program over-sight, communication, budget development, program evaluation, and op-erations. This model placed NTC in the new role of coimplementer, as compared with most other programs (in which the district alone is respon-sible for overseeing and implementing programs).

Second, instead of focusing solely on induction, CNTC uses a series of wraparound services, creating a three-pronged effort focused on develop-ing comprehensive support. The district's chief education officer, Barbara

Eason-Watkins, who led the effort to improve support for new teachers, felt that it was critical to align the support with current district needs, resources, and priorities. After many conversations to identify the areas of alignment that would have most impact on student learning, initiative leaders determined that they would focus on several groups of prekindergarten through eighth grade schools, in the district's instructional areas with the hardest-to-staff schools. Support includes the following:

- *The induction strand:* a mentoring program with full-time release mentors

- *The principal strand:* support for principals focused on assessing and supporting instruction and designed to grow school leaders' understanding of new teachers' needs

- *The literacy strand:* support for the development of literacy instruction (particularly, the implementation of the district's writing curriculum) as well as instructional coaches throughout the system

The induction strand of CNTC was piloted in 2006 in areas 14 and 15 on the south side of Chicago. In 2007, the program expanded to include areas 8 and 13, and in 2008 the program expanded to include area 17 as well as a small high school math pilot. These areas are considered hard to staff, and most schools are low performing. The areas' free and reduced-lunch rate ranges from 89.7 percent to 96.2 percent. The neighborhoods struggle with high crime, high unemployment, and declining home ownership. After looking at the data, including staffing patterns and attrition rates, district leaders determined that these schools were in greatest need of additional support.

The CNTC induction program currently supports approximately 350 teachers in about ninety schools. Incoming Chief Executive Officer Ron Huberman, in concert with Eason-Watkins, has asked CNTC to go to scale. As of 2009–2010, CNTC will be expanded to include almost all new teachers in the Chicago public schools.

Mentors in this strand of the program are released full time to work with first- and second-year teachers. Mentors working with special education teachers support twelve teachers per year, and all other mentors support sixteen teachers per year. As much as possible, mentors are matched with new teachers according to grade level or subject area (or both). Men-

State Policy Context

In 2005, the Joyce Foundation of Chicago supported the New Teacher Center in convening a summit to help three states—Illinois, Ohio, and Wisconsin—assess and support high-quality mentoring and induction. That event brought together a new team in Illinois—the Illinois Induction Policy Team—which included a state agency, a university-based collaborative focused on new teacher induction, union leadership, program directors, NTC policy staff, local funders, and the governor's office.

Building on the energy and connections made at the summit, as well as a growing understanding of the impact of teacher induction in the state, the Illinois team began meeting regularly, revitalizing the commitment to bring high-quality mentoring and induction to Illinois. One result of the team's effort was new state funding for pilot induction programs (now called "state-funded programs") that began to move from buddy programs to designs that meet standards of high quality. Although several earlier efforts were made to improve mentoring in Illinois, this work was the first to succeed in developing programs that included state funding and increased attention to quality standards.

The policy team continues to meet quarterly, has formed an active committee structure based on a multifaceted strategic plan, and is focused on expanding the statewide program in coming years. NTC maintains a strong presence in the state-level activities to inform (and be informed by) the conversations and ongoing legislative efforts for high-quality mentoring.

The Chicago Public Schools, in partnership with Chicago New Teacher Center, applied for and received funding for induction programs in each year of the state grants. It is within this state context that the district committed to expanding its support of new teachers across the city.

tors seek to spend between sixty and ninety minutes, three times a month, helping their new teachers develop strong instructional practice. Their work is guided by the Illinois Professional Teaching Standards and includes the implementation of NTC's Formative Assessment System.

Additional elements of the induction program include a summer institute, monthly professional development seminars for beginning teachers, and an online support network hosted by Yahoogroups. To parallel familiar professional development language in the district, mentors in the CNTC program are referred to as coaches rather than mentors.

THE CHICAGO STORY

New teachers coming to the south side of Chicago are not always prepared for the challenges presented by these neighborhood schools. High transiency rates (topping 30 percent in almost half the schools the program serves), high poverty rates, and racially isolated schools are the norm. In addition, the city's recent murder rate includes a staggering number of student deaths by gun violence. Even when these crimes are not on school property, the issues still find their way into the classroom. In some cases, differences in race, class, and culture mean that teachers are not familiar with the backgrounds of the students; this gap in knowledge sometimes exacerbates the teachers' own discomfort with navigating these new settings successfully.

District leaders soon became aware of the hardships new teachers were facing. After reviewing data on retention, Eason-Watkins argued that "what we learned is that we had a revolving door in many of our communities. We had mentors in many of the schools, but it wasn't sufficient." A study conducted by a community organization a few years earlier had found that the schools in many of Chicago's south side communities were losing new teachers at startling rates. The average turnover of new teachers after five years was peaking at a rate of 73 percent, compared with the national rate of approximately 46 percent.[1] Moreover, the report found that nearly 40 percent of CPS teachers working in schools with high-poverty, minority students leave the school after only one year.

Aware that prior "low-touch" mentoring efforts were not addressing the huge needs of these schools, the district decided to look into developing a program that would provide intensive, more innovative support targeted to new teachers in the area. In addition to mentoring, the district was interested in developing a series of wraparound services that would support integration of the work across the district and improve instruction in all schools.

Mentor selection

Recognizing the importance of creating a strong coaching team, CNTC program leaders created a strong recruitment and selection process. In the start-up year, leaders focused on their current deep professional networks, reaching out personally to exceptional teacher leaders having the skills and potential to be outstanding mentors. When state funding was received, mentoring positions were also posted in district vacancy bulletins. In addition to tapping in to these networks, program leaders actively reached out to award-winning teachers as well as the National Board certified teachers in Chicago.

Many of the strongest coach candidates struggled with the decision to leave the classroom. District leaders and coaches supported the program by finding ways to make their transitions less stressful on their schools and students, and helping them navigate the administrative paperwork that can make leaving the classroom a challenge.

Strong and supportive recruitment allowed program leaders to select a strong caliber of mentors with potential for great leadership. This commitment to quality was an important element, considering that many programs take several years to identify and select the best potential mentors.

The challenge with the Chicago approach will be felt in the scale-up of the initiative. Reaching out to the best educators in the system on a one-to-one level works well on a small scale but will surely be tested as the program expands. Questions about how to ensure quality in the mentor force will undoubtedly arise as program leaders lose their ability to be as personal and selective in their approach.

Area partnerships and principal outreach

Reviewing and building on the lessons learned from program efforts in New York City and knowing the context of Chicago well, program and district leaders chose to have a focused effort to engage and support principals. In deciding how to encourage this type of buy in, the program started with a multipronged effort.

First, program leaders created instructional coaching support for beginning principals so that the CNTC would be seen as a critical friend in developing instructional excellence. Second, they aligned all three components of the program—principal support, literacy, and mentoring—with the work already being accomplished by leaders in each region (what the district refers to as an *area),* which is also where principal supervision sits, so that efforts would be mutually reinforcing and integrated. Third, they intensified training for mentors to reach out to principals in meaningful ways. The strategy was designed and supported by Eason-Watkins and by then CEO Arne Duncan, who had the vision and leverage for ensuring this alignment across the system.

The first of the alignment efforts were reasonably successful. It was acknowledged that most principals did not get the training they needed during their own certification programs to understand how to assess and support new teachers, especially in developing their instruction. Using the Formative Assessment System and other district-developed protocols, the program's leadership coaches (former area leaders and principals selected by the CNTC for their strong instructional development and coaching skills) sought to support new principals in the collection of observation and student data and in the use of reflective conversation and feedback about the data. The new principals seemed open to and appreciative of the leadership-level coaching support, and administrator awareness and support of CNTC's work were quickly expanding.

As the program has developed, CNTC has looked for ways to strategically engage experienced principals. These methods include leading study groups, aligning principal coaching in those schools that have high numbers of new teachers, and coleading an area-based pilot of Charlotte Danielson's Framework for Teaching, which has included a strong focus on observation and feedback.

The second effort to align support of the CNTC program with area efforts was potentially the most powerful and successful aspect in meeting the specified goals.[2] Based on NTC's experience in New York City, Chicago program leadership knew that alignment would be critical to the success of the program. As with Chicago, in New York City's public schools, support for new teachers comes from a number of staff who have various roles. Because there was limited communication between those staffers (literacy coaches, mentors, principals, university liaisons, etc.), new teachers often reported feeling confused by the many ideological frameworks, messages, and expectations. In some cases, the support was so disconnected that new teachers felt overwhelmed and frustrated, suggesting that support was diluted, or perhaps even counterproductive, because of the confusion.

To achieve stronger alignment from the outset, Chicago program leaders set clear expectations that any initiative would be rolled out in collaboration and with strong communication with the area leaders (whom the district calls AIOs, or area instructional officers). Program leaders have gone a great distance in meeting these expectations by building strong rapport with each AIO, codesigning and implementing training, generating regular communication and feedback, and serving as critical friends and thought leaders. Program staffers attend all AIO principal meetings and work closely with AIOs to ensure that there is alignment between all materials, training, and messaging that goes out to educators. One area leader says, "We are working constantly on keeping the message the same. Part of it is the language; a lot of it is that we are aligning on strategies."

Parallel with the program's area work, the district's Office of Instructional Design and Assessment (IDA) was working to align the multiple coaching initiatives that touched schools. IDA invited CNTC to join this discussion, which became multiple conversations, retreats, and design meetings to help create a theory of action for coaching and to identify key actions for coaches, including literacy, math, and other instructional coaches who were released from teaching duties to support schools and teachers directly. It became clear that the New Teacher Center tools and protocols could be a source of coherence among the coaches, and in 2007, IDA asked CNTC to help train and support in-school instructional coaches across the district.

Using customized training and working in close partnership with IDA, program leaders helped roll out the districtwide coaching initiative. Specifically, program leaders (working with staff from NTC) trained in-school instructional coaches in key pieces of the Formative Assessment System (FAS), including the use of NTC tools: the Collaborative Assessment Log, Selective Scripting, Analyzing Student Work, and Lesson Planning A and B. These protocols and tools were modified slightly to meet the specific context of the various CPS initiatives.

Training for this group focused on developing a common language for identifying, assessing, and supporting high-quality instruction, using protocols as entry points for building educator capacity to provide high-quality instruction, and developing language that is critical to establishing the kind of successful rapport that allows for significant educator growth. In the second year, the program held forums for the coaches of coaches, creating a sustained opportunity to build coaching capacity, solve problems, and continue the efforts to create coherence in coaching initiatives.

The third strategy was marked by a concerted effort to enhance internal program training and support for building strong principal relationships. Although NTC training typically includes a segment on working with site-based administrators, CNTC worked to augment such training by focusing on the issue regularly in mentor forums, developing protocols for principal interaction, and prioritizing messages about and actions affecting the key role a principal plays in a new teacher's success.

The outcomes from this three-pronged effort have been promising but not perfect. The efforts to align support with AIOs have had the most positive impact with principals. When there are strong relationships between program staff and AIOs, this positive push helps create strong relationships with principals in that area, and messages are truly aligned. Leaders conclude that these relationships and the specific efforts to align strategies have been critical for establishing buy in, in part because AIOs set the expectations for principals.

When program coaching is prioritized by the area, the reception from principals is more successful. It becomes a mutually reinforcing strategy that, most observers agree, outstrips the significant time and resource investments necessary for true collaboration. One coach explained, "It's key to work in partnership schools where you have the support of the AIO . . . where you have that buy in already present. Without them, it's like pulling teeth to get the support of the principals . . . I have to really pour it on . . . they think we're spies, they don't know what we're doing, who we are . . . and it's so much more work to gain their trust or even interest in the work we're doing. I'd much prefer to work only in partnership schools."

Program leaders see successful partnerships in the majority of school settings that they work in. They credit this high level of collaboration to the visionary leadership, openness, and charismatic personalities of the AIOs. The relationships and types of activities are different in each area. With each relationship, a new collaboration is shaped based on the needs and current initiatives in play.

Anecdotal evidence suggests that the level of ownership by AIOs is directly correlated with the level of ownership of principals in that area. Program leaders believe they have been able to create deep seeds of shared ownership of goals and outcomes for the district, specifically because they have had the opportunity to work with a cadre of visionary AIOs who are open to this level of partnership.

One of the challenges of this approach, however, has been the focus on relationship building and contextualization of support strategies. Program staffers have succeeded in developing trust and a shared sense of ownership in each area because they have spent a great deal of time creating those relationships and identifying how to integrate strategies appropriately.

CNTC is currently partnering only with five areas. As the program expands into new areas across Chicago, the ability to create the relationships necessary to engender deep collaboration will be tested. This challenge is in part a function of time, because limited program staff will not always be able to spend the time necessary to foster these relationships. And in part it is a function of capacity and will; some AIOs may have less interest in and knowledge of how to transcend their own priorities to accommodate and collaborate based on a new vision of educational success. Program leaders are exploring strategies for building infrastructure that can support this type of collaboration at scale, but it depends in part on continued messages from senior Chicago Public School leadership in making this partnership a priority.

The issue of collaboration, however, has turned out to be more complex than some leaders anticipated. Although thoughtful and deep collaboration has been penetrating the top layers of the program (a success that many programs have yet to achieve), this seamless integration of strategies has yet to fully penetrate the on-the-ground layers of support in schools.

The district invested significant funding on NTC training for literacy coaches. The training was extremely well received, with high ratings across the board and requests for ongoing training, which has continued. Participants particularly underscored the excitement of developing a common language to describe high-quality instruction and being provided with tools and approaches to help guide teacher practice forward. Program and district leaders consider the training a significant success and a model for the ways districts can consider strategies for alignment. As they scale, program leaders are now exploring how this alignment can explicitly translate into increased collaboration between mentors and literacy coaches in the same schools.

Mentors say that the collaboration they have with literacy coaches is somewhat easier because of the knowledge they share, but true collaboration in aligning support for new teachers (as in the case of the AIOs) is more dependent on time, personality, and interest in developing shared ownership of a new teacher's success. One coach asserted, "I got along with a few of the coaches really well. Those were the ones that gave me their time . . . at first I think it was because of our relationship more than anything . . . then, after they started figuring out that it helped the teachers for us to think strategically as a team . . . then they became invested in the process."

Without clear expectations and protocols for ways to collaborate successfully on a regular basis, mentors and coaches were left to find their own ways to work together. Coaches note that this ad hoc approach has resulted in deep collaboration in some places, where mentors and coaches prioritize time to think creatively together, but that type of relationship tends to be idiosyncratic and isolated. In two regional areas, the program has worked explicitly to create more opportunities for shared coaching and learning experiences between induction and literacy coaches, with the hope of piloting new ways to continue to build alignment.

Finally, the additional support for mentors to interact with principals has been well received by the mentors. They have expressed a great deal of appreciation for the ongoing reflection and conversations that support these efforts and feel that their skills continue to develop. With the additional support, these mentors likely have climbed further up the learning curve than mentors in some other programs.

However, they continue to cite challenges that ring true in most programs. Some suggest that there is a transition in their own thinking about how they interact with principals. This transition sometimes inhibits confidence in securing time with the principal or advocating to ensure that administrators make new teacher support a priority. One coach disclosed, "In my school, you didn't just go up and treat the principal as a colleague.

They're your boss, you know? Now, because of my experience and working with so many schools, I know I have important and good knowledge about instruction . . . it's just taken me a while to get out of the mind-set that I can speak with them as a peer, you know? And it would be received OK. I think some other of the coaches are also having trouble making that leap."

Other coaches say that principals are too busy to take sufficient time to meet with them to learn about the types of strategies they are enacting with their new teachers. Some argue that the confidentiality between mentors and new teachers makes administrators uneasy, because they are some-times uncomfortable with not being told the specifics of their teachers' progress. And most coaches acknowledge that they have not had enough time with principals to ensure a comprehensive understanding of the For-mative Assessment System, teaching standards, or components of the pro-gram that make the mentoring effective. Some of the coaches report being successful in building the principal's knowledge on some of these pieces, but again, this success is more idiosyncratic than systematic.

Interestingly, even though many principals have a strong awareness of the CNTC through the multifaceted programming and AIO leadership, a few continue to be underinformed or frustrated by their lack of partici-pation in mentor selection. As one former administrator says, "When the program first rolled out, I felt out of the loop. Teachers in this program look to coaches as the first line of support, not the administrators. That's hard at first . . . but then once I understood the impact of the program, I agree it is the way it should be. But it took me a while to get there."

CNTC has worked to take administrators from this state of low engage-ment or frustration to a state of understanding and encouragement for the program. Each year, the three-pronged strategy for administrator buy in has continued to engender in principals a collective sense of excitement and support for the program, and administrators see coaches as allies and cata-lysts for the change that they envision. There is still a fair amount of work to be done to get all principals to this place. Program leaders will continue to measure implementation and modify strategies to achieve this goal.

Engaged communication

Much of Chicago's success in implementing all aspects of its program is driven by a strong communication strategy. In many programs, activities and goals tend to focus on one part of the district system. Whether it's human resources, the curriculum and instruction office, elementary or high school education, technology, or another area, departmental initiatives tend to remain isolated in scope, with only occasional bits of information being shared across divisions. CNTC program leaders have taken the opposite strategy, making it a top priority to link with all other elements of the Chicago Public Schools system.

This endeavor has been an intensive and time-consuming process. Program leaders meet regularly with district leaders, making presentations and providing data on program successes and challenges. They work regularly with AIOs to align the work and develop messages that ensure consistency with each area initiative. They attend every principals meeting, something that helps them to be seen as an ongoing and invested presence. These meetings also help inform their work. They develop a better understanding of the current needs and issues faced by principals, which in turn increases entry points for further alignment.

Program leaders also provide regular updates to and facilitate an online community with educators throughout the system. This Web-based resource provides more than information on the specific programs of CNTC; it also gives educators a venue to receive information about resources, instructional strategies, logistics, social issues, and anything else they might have questions about. The Web site posts nearly one hundred messages and responses each month. Leaders suggest that this kind of communication helps them take the pulse of the schools and stay connected with new initiatives, issues, and general feelings about school-related efforts as they arise.

In addition to internal communication, program staffers have taken one step farther and tried to invoke broad-based external support for the endeavors. Working with reporters and editorial writers to educate them on the reform efforts and the needs of new teachers has paid off, with a number of articles and editorial placements in the Chicago press helping highlight the benefits of intensive teacher mentoring in the district. Bringing in funders from the earliest stages of the initiative and keeping them informed of successes and growth areas have ensured that CNTC has the additional funding necessary to innovate and expand programs. Funders have thus far included the Joyce Foundation, the Arie & Ida Crown Memorial, LISC/Chicago, Lloyd A. Fry Foundation, Steans Family Foundation, and the Boeing Company.

Through work with the Illinois Induction Policy Team and the NTC Policy Division, program leadership has continued to support the design and implementation of a statewide mentoring program. Because the NTC Policy Division was funded to facilitate the convening of statewide Illinois agencies and leaders to redesign teacher mentoring, emerging CNTC leaders serve as a critical resource to inform and develop relationships with state leaders interested in raising the quality of mentoring in the state. This effort has supported strong relationships with key stakeholders, including program leaders across the state, the Illinois New Teacher Collaborative (which has program oversight for pilot programs), state AFT and NEA leaders, and the Illinois State Department of Education.

By tapping in to networks of education stakeholders outside the district, CNTC has significantly broadened knowledge of and interest in the work. District leadership fully endorses the work internally and externally when discussing the future of Chicago public schools. Administrators hear aligned messages about the programs and regularly talk about and interact with CNTC. National and local reporters promote the importance of the work, generating excitement for the program from state policy circles to local advocates. CNTC represents a successful effort in the field to build communication that supports the political will for the work, and maintaining this energy will be a critical factor in the sustainability of the program over the long term.

Alignment

Underlying all these communication activities has been a conspicuous effort to create what leaders suggest is an integral component of success: aligned messaging. Program, district, and area leaders all note that the alignment of messaging has been critical to the success of the program. When education stakeholders (district leaders, media, state policy makers, and principals and teachers) receive clear and consistent information about various instructional initiatives, the initiatives become easier to understand and integrate into regular school processes—and political leverage is generated to prioritize the implementation. One leader offered a simple, critical insight: "The more you can get similar messages out . . . the easier it is for people to buy in."

This alignment counters the typical approach seen in large urban school systems, where principals are responsible for juggling multiple initiatives (state, district, and other) with little insight or guidance in how to thoughtfully prioritize the many mandates coming down. This difficulty is sometimes hypothesized as a significant factor in the soaring rates of principal turnover.

A critical element of message alignment, leaders say, is to understand what you can negotiate in your own priorities to reinforce and support other ideas and initiatives. This trade-off highlights an important issue that sometimes challenges the success of the initiatives. For example, CNTC program leadership has noticed that even though the level of excitement for the work is always high, this enthusiasm has not necessarily translated into increased support for coaches or new teachers in schools—at least not to the extent originally hoped. They suggest that so much time has been spent on aligning messages with current system protocols and in integrating tools to support instructional success that some of the emphasis specifically on new teacher support has become diluted.

Leaders say that this general tension was anticipated from the beginning of the initiative. They assert that there is a fine line between maintaining integrity of program components and aligning programs with other major initiatives. Although it can be challenging to walk this line, leaders say it is ultimately worth the investment when in return you engender the type of buy in and ownership that allow the work to thrive. Ultimately, ensuring message alignment has allowed CNTC to penetrate myriad layers of the CPS system and become a powerful force for change in the district and the state.

IMPACT OF WORKING CONDITIONS

In developing messages that are truly aligned, CNTC leaders have realized that some critical messages are missing, raising significant obstacles to the work. One coach observes, "Our principals support the induction program. They get that new teachers need support. There's just not an understanding that there is a role for the school as well."

Although high-quality mentoring has been proven as a critical element for improving retention of new teachers, it has also been shown that the conditions of a school have a significant impact on teachers' successes and the decision to remain in teaching. For example, if a new teacher does not receive support from her administrator, if she is feeling isolated from her colleagues, if other teachers receive resources that she does not, if student discipline policies are not enforced, if she is asked to take on all the extra noninstructional duties that veteran teachers don't want, and if the school culture breeds negativity instead of rigor, energy, and excitement about teaching and learning, then the likelihood of the new teacher's staying in that school is slim, no matter how wonderful her work with a mentor is.

CNTC leaders realize that if the program is to be effective in reaching retention goals and ultimately impacting student learning, they will need to develop strategies to address these conditions in meaningful ways. Leaders acknowledge that principal certification and training programs generally have limited focus on how to assign and support new teachers in ways that ensure their success. Given CNTC's knowledge and experience in this field and its entry point with new principals in CPS, this seems a natural place to take the initiative. Leaders are devising a strategy that includes working with principals to create conditions that will lead to the success of new teachers (and ultimately all teachers).

OUTCOMES

CNTC has tracked its own retention data, among other measures of success. In fall 2008, 85 percent of the first- and second-year teachers supported by CNTC returned to the district to teach. In addition, CNTC tracks completion rates—the percentage of teachers who finish a school year. As of this writing, that rate is 95 percent, in schools where vacancy rates traditionally topped 15 percent during the school year. Comparable retention or completion data is not available from Chicago Public Schools, and that makes direct comparisons challenging, but the district has been pleased with these strong results. CNTC continues to expand its ability to collect, analyze, and report on important data regarding retention, teacher demographics, teacher development, and, eventually, student learning.

LESSONS LEARNED

This model of program delivery is NTC's first exploration as implementer within a large urban district. Some NTC efforts were successful beyond expectations. Some hurdles were higher than NTC anticipated. Some questions emerged that perplexed NTC leaders, and some solutions emerged that delighted us. From all these experiences have emerged insights and lessons learned that provide a powerful platform for supporting districts in future efforts. An outline of the lessons learned is provided next.

Quality first, and then scale

Piloting the program in two areas first, as opposed to going to scale immediately, has helped the program reach a level of excellence in its initial phases. Mentor selection was rigorous, strategic, and intentional, ensuring a very high caliber of candidates. Program leaders developed relationships with AIOs based on one-on-one communication, and collaboration thrived. Program leaders prioritized participation and communication with all administrators, generating a significant level of buy in from principals. These elements ensured the quality of the program from the outset and will support its sustainability over time.

This type of approach is even more powerful when juxtaposed with programs that go to full scale (districtwide) immediately and tend not to perform as well in mentor selection, collaboration, and communication in the initial years. Many such programs eventually find success in these areas, but typically it takes a number of years to establish the level of success that CNTC has achieved during its start-up.

Because of the quality and broad support for the program, Chicago Public Schools has committed to expanding the programs over the next several years. This plan presents interesting challenges. Although starting small has enabled the program to be ahead of the curve during implementation, there are many questions about how it will maintain the integrity and quality of the program as it scales up over time.

How will the program continue to identify and select the highest-quality educators to be mentors? How will the program maintain the level of collaboration with each area as economies of scale begin to overshadow time for relationship building? How will the model communication plan be affected when more program time is spent on the complex operations of implementing a full-scale program? Program and district leaders continue to grapple with these questions and explore innovative solutions that will be tested in the coming years.

Make communication a priority

The Chicago story represents one of the most successful models of program communication that NTC has seen. One of the most significant factors in the district's success is its visibility in multiple settings. Program leaders participate regularly in key stakeholder forums, including principal meetings, AIO meetings, district leadership meetings in various departments (human resources, content and curriculum, chief education office), funder networking, policy meetings, professional development rollout meetings, media forums, and schools. By making themselves a consistent presence in all circles, CNTC leaders have entered conversations to support initiatives outside the scope of their program—and in return receive support and opportunities to push the system forward. In addition, by facilitating a districtwide Web site to connect people and resources, CNTC stays in touch with educators throughout the city. This proactive stance has helped CNTC develop a communication plan that is strategic, relevant, and aligned with program goals.

How well will the organization sustain this level of time investment as the program scales up? It is clear that districts interested in maintaining an aligned strategy for reform should heed the lesson that sharing information across divisions and identifying opportunities for collaboration across areas are critical elements for success.

Navigate alignment top-down and bottom-up

Chicago provides an exceptional example of alignment between its regional supervisors (AIOs) and CNTC program leadership, and this alignment leads to consistency in messaging and initiative rollout from the top layers of the system down to the school and classroom level. The district has also gone farther than most urban districts by advocating for training not only for mentors but also for instructional and literacy coaches across the city. Although this thoughtful approach addresses alignment, the implementation has not yet yielded full collaboration at the school level, so additional thought is needed.

Examples might include developing protocols for collaboration by support providers, modeling what collaboration looks like on the ground, and regularly bringing together instructional and literacy coaches with new teacher mentors to share data, collaboratively brainstorm strategies for support, and develop a professional community of practice. Program and district leaders are also exploring ways to support and advance training for principals, focusing on how to use their coaching resources strategically. Program and district leaders continue to identify new and emerging ideas for implementing best practices that can be seen and felt where it counts: in the classroom.

Create a balance between focus and alignment

NTC has an unyielding and specific focus on new teacher development. The decision by Chicago's program and district leaders to broaden the scope of the work to focus on literacy coaching and principal development (in addition to concerted efforts to align messaging with other initiatives) has created a deviation from the NTC model.

The Chicago model has proven to be effective in some ways and problematic in others. Because of this strategy, CNTC's expertise in supporting teacher quality has penetrated many areas of the system that might not otherwise have been touched. For example, the CNTC approach supports alignment of strategies so that educators do not receive mixed messages about instructional frameworks and practices. In addition, CNTC has enjoyed broad access to conversations throughout the Chicago public schools, allowing officials to push institutional change in many areas.

This trade-off suggests a tension that should be noted by district leaders and reform effort implementers. Focus on an initiative and interest in meeting stated benchmarks should never overshadow the need for alignment of strategies, collaboration, and cross-divisional goal-setting. However, too much focus on alignment and collaboration can undermine the potency of any given initiative. CNTC continues to try to find the balance between these two strategies and will know more about how to navigate this tension as the program continues to evolve.

Address working conditions in schools

Although the initiative has not yet begun, research from the Consortium on Chicago School Reform clearly indicates that to address new teacher development successfully, a concerted effort is needed to address the working conditions in schools. The best mentoring program can't keep teachers if the working conditions are terrible. CNTC, given its expertise in addressing the needs of new teachers and its ongoing work with principals, is positioning itself to take on this critical next level of work. Supporting principals in understanding the importance of giving new teachers developmentally appropriate classrooms, modifying their workloads so that they can take the time to learn their craft, and ensuring that they have emotional, logistical, and *instructional* support (as opposed to evaluation alone) will pay huge dividends to the district and to students most in need of an excellent education.

This effort parallels a new initiative of the New Teacher Center, which surveys educators statewide to help define and develop plans to address working conditions in the schools. A focus on working conditions gives hope that someday soon all schools will be able to prioritize instructional learning over logistical processes and tradition.

PART III

Conclusions and Recommendations

8
—

Analyzing Trends: Strategies Honed, Questions Raised, Levers for Change

Each of the case studies presented in this book tells a story tied closely to the context of the school district. The history, political landscape, size, and culture of each system have dictated, in large part, the successes and challenges it has experienced in implementing high-quality mentoring. Nevertheless, when looking at the four sites (Durham, Chicago, Boston, and New York City), NTC has observed patterns that seem to transcend the context of the system. Some trends are reinforced by emerging research; others rub up against existing evidence and challenge us to think more deeply about what successful mentoring looks like in urban settings; still others raise questions that invite further exploration. Within these patterns, however, lie lessons that have implications for educational leaders seeking to build high-quality mentoring programs and implement comprehensive human capital strategies.

These lessons may serve as guideposts that help leaders focus their energy and prioritize their funding, navigate complex systems and avoid hidden obstacles, and, ultimately, create strong partnerships that help new teachers succeed. This chapter highlights key insights drawn from the four cases and validated by the NTC's two decades of experience in the field.

STRATEGIES THAT ARE WORKING ACROSS DISTRICTS

Each of the case study sites highlighted in this book has introduced innovations on the typical NTC program and in doing so has begun to develop model policies and promising practices that are sure to have strong impacts on new teachers, students—and mentors! These districts might be considered on the cutting edge of mentoring efforts, and their successes cannot be overstated. Here we discuss some of the key achievements and most creative new strategies that we believe epitomize what high-quality induction should look like in schools.

Recruitment and selection of mentors

One of the most powerful bottom-line conclusions of the case studies is the criticality of recruiting and selecting the right people to be mentors—and the power of school districts to be successful in this endeavor. When mentors represent a cadre of the most talented educators in the system—with exceptional relationship-building skills and capacities that apply to and beyond the classroom—their work with new teachers and schools can help improve student learning across the system. Programs gain recognition and build power as the reputation of these mentors grows and as stakeholders realize and tap into the potential of these human resources to transform instruction.

Yet when a lack of time or funding inhibits a comprehensive and rigorous mentor recruitment and selection process, and when the mentors do not represent the most exceptional educators or don't have strong interpersonal skills, the program likely will not accomplish its mission. Mentors will not be viewed as critical forces for supporting new teacher development, and their voices will not be as powerful in supporting school change. It is therefore critical that districts focus first, and primarily, on getting the right people to be mentors. Unfortunately, there are myriad systemic and historical obstacles to achieving success in recruitment and selection.

Most veteran teachers and administrators have never experienced instructional mentoring, and, when programs begin to recruit, many potential candidates may be reluctant to apply. Others may not apply for the mentor position because of fears for their job security; they may assume that a new initiative is "another fly-by-night program" that may not last more than a year or two. Historically, the profession has offered few leadership opportunities for talented teachers to step out of the classroom into new roles; as a result, they may be cautious before taking the risk of leaving the classroom and a school they like. In addition, school administrators understandably are not eager to encourage their best teachers to apply for mentor positions if they do not see a direct benefit for their school.

Despite these potential obstacles, the case studies show that exceptional candidates can be recruited and selected in the first year of a program when recruitment efforts are intentional, strategic, and aggressive. In Chicago, program officials were well-connected instructional leaders who had worked in Chicago public schools for many years and were familiar with many outstanding classroom teachers in the initiative's targeted south side schools, and they made a concerted effort to reach out to people within their existing internal networks. The program started small, with fewer than a dozen mentors. This modest start-up allowed program leaders to research and reach out to educators who had achieved distinction in their teaching careers (teachers of the year, National Board certified teachers, etc.).

Durham's successful recruitment efforts were the result, in part, of high-level collaboration among the superintendent, department leaders, and the broad-based program ownership. This multilevel public support added cachet to the program and caught the attention of some of the schools' top educators. It was bolstered by the superintendent's decision to review each mentor candidate's longitudinal test score data to ensure that each had a track record of success with students of all backgrounds. Although somewhat controversial, this decision emphasized the value placed on a mentor candidate's effective teaching practice and the importance of selecting high-quality teachers to usher in and support the next generation.

Even though they did not fill all positions by the start of the school year, Durham program leaders did not relax their standards for mentor selection. After reviewing the first pool of mentor applicants, program leaders decided that many of the candidates had not demonstrated the desired level of instructional practice. Rather than lower their standards, they decided not to fill all positions and reposted the positions mid-year. (Boston also chose not to fill all mentor positions until it felt that all mentors met its high standard of excellence.) Durham's decision fueled the program's emerging reputation for holding extremely high expectations and encouraged even more top educators to apply for the positions.

Principal engagement

Principals are important, both in the professional life of new teachers and in the work of mentors. It is critical that principals be engaged in any mentoring initiative, because each new teacher is striving to be successful in the context of a specific school. Just as an effective mentor should tailor support to the assessed developmental needs of each novice, so too should mentors and mentoring programs be attentive and responsive to the needs of a given school's context and the vision, instructional focus, and priorities set by that school's principal.

If the principal's vision for the school is not aligned with the focus of the work between mentors and new teachers, then mentors and principals may work at cross purposes and undermine a new teacher's opportunities to succeed. Unfortunately, in a number of programs, there is a gap between the mentors' work and the principals' visions for instruction. Many factors underlie this gap, including limited communication with administrators, lack of administrator participation in the selection of mentors, and lack of clarity regarding the mentor's role, as well as misunderstandings about ways a mentor can communicate and interact with a principal while maintaining a confidential relationship with new teachers.

In New York City, many of these factors meant that school administrators had limited knowledge of and interest in the program. The consequences were felt as the city moved to a new autonomous school system, and only a small portion of administrators understood the quality of the instructional mentoring that was taking place in their classrooms. As a result, New York has moved to a mentoring program that is designed and implemented by principals. Some principals have drawn on and applied the knowledge and expertise of the instructional mentors who had been deployed at their sites, and others have reverted to the traditional buddy system.

Building on the work in New York, the Durham, Chicago, and Boston programs have sought to develop more-structured bridges between program leaders, mentors, and principals. Chicago has developed a principal training and support program. Chicago New Teacher Center program leaders collaborate with area instructional officers, who are responsible for supervising principals, and attend nearly all principal meetings in the district. The effort has led to a reasonably high level of principal awareness of the CNTC's work as well as interest expressed by principals in the strategies and protocols used by mentors to move teacher practice forward.

Durham's approach is supported by the program's structure. Because most mentors work in only one or two schools, they have time to interact with each principal, develop a relationship, and collaborate in supporting the new teachers. Without breaking confidentiality, mentors and principals can support each other in a coordinated tag-team approach to accelerate new teachers' learning. Principals report that because of the sometimes overwhelming day-to-day demands of their jobs, they often don't have time to focus on instructional leadership as much as they would like. They see the mentor as a critical ally in moving that important work forward.

The Boston program uses a multipronged strategy for principal engagement. By involving principals in matching mentors to new teachers, the program gives school leaders a voice in who works in their schools. Program leaders have also implemented a knowledge-building strategy, including the use of toolkits and professional development training to enable principals to build their own capacity to create working conditions that support new teachers. The Boston program also uses these materials and training to clarify the mentor's role and articulate the confidentiality agreements between mentors and new teachers. School leaders who understand the power and importance of new teachers having close, confidential relationships with mentors have been asked to be the voice of the policy. These outreach efforts have helped create broader support for the program throughout the community.

Strengthening the links between mentors and principals and appropriately engaging site administrators in the mentoring work continue to be ongoing challenges for all the programs. High rates of principal turnover in urban settings mean that program leaders must continuously communicate the features and impact of mentoring. As a result of competing priorities, many principals feel they do not have time to meet with or learn about the strategies used by mentors. In other cases, principals are not well supported in becoming strong, confident instructional leaders who fully understand how to build teacher effectiveness and who can embrace collaborative approaches to the instructional support of their new teachers.

In truth, the historical context of mentoring programs—the prevalence of traditional buddy systems—means that without new knowledge, principals may continue to feel skeptical about the quality and potential impact of mentoring. Effective program leaders work to subvert this kind of thinking by embracing principals as key allies in the support of new teachers and developing a variety of methods for engaging them meaningfully and strategically in the initiative.

Program communication

Like any systemwide initiative, mentoring programs benefit when everyone is on the same page. However, multiple layers of bureaucracy, departments working in isolation from one another, competing initiatives with different leaders, methods, and visions all add to the complexity of institutional alignment. Getting everyone on the same page requires effective, ongoing communication. The Chicago case highlights an array of effective communication strategies.

Chicago NTC leaders have made communication a top priority, and their investment of time and resources is paying off. By using proactive strategies to reach out to internal and external stakeholders, by prioritizing messages that link initiatives, and by sanctioning time to identify and follow up on opportunities to collaborate, the program has become a respected, relied-upon resource for instructional support in Chicago public schools. CNTC leaders are consistently present at meetings of all initiatives related to teacher development. They have created an online new teacher and mentor resource to support information sharing, and they work hard to ensure that all messaging includes other instructional initiatives and frameworks being implemented in the system. Externally, CNTC leaders have built relationships and share information with local, state, and federal policy makers, teachers unions, media, community organizations, and others who are interested in but, to some extent, removed from the system.

Partnering with teacher unions

Teacher unions and associations are critical partners in the work. There is a natural partnership between mentoring programs and teachers associations, because working conditions (a traditional union issue) are an important component in a new teacher's decision to remain in a district. As district office and program leadership regularly transitions and perhaps even moves on to other districts, support by local teacher associations and unions can often serve as a strong, stabilizing force for programs.

Forward-thinking teacher associations recognize that new teachers are their future membership and want to engage in efforts that support their professional success and well-being. Without associations' full support and ownership, efforts to implement programs can be bumpy, surface-level, and ineffective. In addition, their ability to negotiate language into bargaining agreements regarding high-quality mentoring and support for ongoing teacher development positions them as potential gatekeepers to program sustainability.

The partnership between Boston Public Schools and the Boston Teachers Union has helped solidify support and increase investment in the program throughout the school community. The union's and district's mutual interest in supporting the program has fostered successful negotiations despite time line and political challenges. Both the union and the district felt that negotiating language in the contract was important for ensuring successful implementation and sustainability of the program's priorities.

The New York City case represents a unique partnership between the district and the union, one that developed despite a backdrop of contentious bargaining relations. Because the need to address retention issues appealed to both district and union leadership, the collaboration moved forward during a tumultuous bargaining year. This natural pairing was fostered, in part, by the existence of a strong professional development unit within the UFT that was jointly funded by state, local, and union funds. The UFT Teachers Center had a history of providing training for mentors and was, from the start, interested in partnering with district program directors to form teams to improve teaching and learning support for new teachers. When teacher associations see teacher development as a union priority, mentoring programs form a natural context for district–union partnerships.

Strong program leadership

Steadfast and innovative leadership characterizes successful programs. Strong program leaders, like strong principals, can influence the mentoring team's vision, the success of a program's implementation, and the success of the individuals who mentor and ultimately become instructional leaders.

Often, mentor program leadership is assigned to an overloaded central office administrator as one more duty, or to a teacher leader on assignment without administrative authority or access to high-level colleagues. That practice is detrimental. Mentor program directors, who oversee all aspects of mentor programs, need a range of skills and knowledge. At the first level, program directors must manage all program logistics and operations, including identifying, releasing, matching, training, and monitoring interactions between mentors and new teachers. But directors must also have concrete knowledge of what constitutes effective instruction and what it will take to build new teacher capacity to provide effective instruction. They must understand how to build and model a community of learners that inspires its members to seek instructional excellence and challenges them to move beyond their comfort levels and historical contexts.

For example, wise program leaders know that many mentors likely have never experienced the sort of instructional mentoring relationship they are expected to forge with their beginning teachers, and few have engaged in thoughtful learning communities focused on one's personal practice. As a result, program directors must be strong facilitators of professional learning communities and effective coaches who tailor support for mentors individually using data-based, just-in-time strategies. Program directors must hold on to their vision for mentoring excellence while selflessly empowering mentors to take the lead in implementing and transforming that vision.

Most of their time is spent supporting mentors to become as effective as possible, but these talented leaders must also navigate the political landscapes of their urban school systems, collect and use many types of data, document their programs' results, and articulate the benefits of the program—and at the same time meet the needs and demands of the many competing priorities of district leaders. Program directors need to be multifaceted, talented, exceptional instructional leaders who understand not only how to create instructional change at the classroom level but also how to create and sustain change at the school and district levels. Just like the mentors they support, these leaders need to be carefully chosen, supported in their own development, and then provided with ample time to lead effectively.

In the four cases presented here, the leaders were empowered to lead, had the trust of their supervisors, and enjoyed the authority to make critical program decisions. These strong leaders inspired their colleagues (up, down, and across the system) and built the capacity of the mentors they led.

They identified mentors who not only had outstanding skills in mentoring but also exhibited the capability and knowledge to innovate and link mentoring to other elements of the system. As a result, mentors became key agents of change at the classroom, school, and district levels. In Durham, mentor leaders use data from the NTC Teaching and Learning Conditions survey to support school change in ways that help their new teachers, as well as their veteran colleagues, thrive.[1] In Chicago, mentor leaders support new mentors in their development and facilitate literacy instruction for school leaders and leadership teams around the city. In New York, mentor leaders have become lead instructional mentors and are responsible for training new mentors and providing professional development regarding teaching standards. In Boston, mentor leaders cofacilitate training and developing new avenues of professional development for mentors and new teachers.

Disseminating professional teaching standards

Professional teaching standards (PTS) that articulate the specific elements of high-quality instruction are an essential element of mentoring. Often, however, these standards remain exclusively in the context of a mentor–teacher relationship. Disseminating the use of professional standards throughout a system helps build a common language, and framework, for assessing and supporting instructional progress. When evaluation systems and teacher development initiatives are aligned, when principals and teachers (new and veteran) share a common professional language, when novices and veterans embrace the same vision of best practice—that's when systems can create synergy in service of a teacher's development and student success.

As New York's mentoring program shifted to the school sites, program leaders recognized the value of building broad knowledge of professional teaching standards, a core component of their full-release mentoring model. Program leaders identified almost seventy lead instructional mentors to assist these site-based efforts and then charged them with building knowledge of how to integrate and use teaching standards to support real change in instructional practice throughout the school community.

The dissemination of teaching standards throughout New York schools has also been aided by the decision to include elements of the standards in one of the primary assessments used to evaluate schools. Principals use the document to focus on instructional improvement at the school and classroom level. But the district's decision to have former mentors serve as the ambassadors for disseminating knowledge about the NTC Continuum and PTS means that the information is penetrating the system through the lens of teacher development and formative assessment, and not high-stakes, summative evaluation. The lead instructional mentors demonstrate the use of professional standards via conversations, strategies, and protocols that help mentors and principals tailor support for new teachers and classroom observations that lead to instructional growth.

Building relationships

One of the most persistent (though least policy amenable) trends running through all cases is the importance of relationship building. From Chicago New Teacher Center's focus on building rapport with the leads in each area, to Durham mentors' focus on building trusting relationships with principals and coaches in each school, to the Boston New Teacher Development program's collaborative relationship with the Boston Teacher Residency program, to the structural relationship between New York's lead instructional mentors and network team staff, the result seems to be the same: reform efforts are most successful when there are strong, trusting individual relationships and a shared vision for success. This goes beyond perfunctory collaboration to a deep respect and appreciation for one another's goals and a personal desire to support one another's work—even when it means compromise or sacrifice.

A program can consider a number of practices to develop strong relationships. First, institutions should pick mentors, program leaders, and other stakeholders wisely by focusing on candidates who are not only open to partnership but also committed to it. District leaders should focus on identifying those who are flexible, empathic, proactive practitioners who can see the big picture as well as their own agenda, and who are persistent enough to work through breakdowns in communication, turf challenges, and other issues that historically plague collaboration.

Second, and likely more difficult, is making the institutional commitment of resources and time for individuals to meet regularly (formally and informally). In this way, people can get to know one another and develop an appreciation for each other as human beings engaged in the difficult work of teacher development and educational reform. The chance to get to know one another helps develop understanding, respect, and support for everyone's professional efforts.

Finally, institutions (and programs) need to set expectations that strong, collaborative, professional relationships are prized and then model the behaviors and provide the structures that help foster those relationships, both institutionally and individually. Programs can do well by providing and facilitating protocols that engage colleagues in looking at complementary and shared goals, in examining data that have implications across programs, in helping craft a shared vision, or in together determining next steps that extend beyond their own agenda.

IMPORTANT QUESTIONS RAISED

The innovative strategies engaged by the four case study sites in this book have provided hope and promise for unleashing the power of school districts to truly support new teacher success and, ultimately, effectiveness. However, as is the case in most efforts that seek to reflect on what is working, we arrive at more questions than answers. The most powerful aspect of this reflective exercise, the writing of this book, is that we may finally be starting to ask the right questions. The challenges and questions discussed here represent some of the core issues that need to be dissected, analyzed, and addressed before mentoring programs can realize their fullest potential—and before human capital strategies (and all efforts that seek to improve educator effectiveness) can be realized.

School-based generalist mentors

Some research suggests that pairing mentors with new teachers having similar subject-matter knowledge is a desirable condition for effective mentoring. NTC strongly advocates for subject-matter matching between mentors and new teachers wherever feasible. Yet the Durham program has successfully taken a generalist approach to mentoring and, in doing so, has challenged us to think about the trade-offs and opportunities that occur when mentors are sufficiently qualified to take a broader perspective to the work.

Durham mentors are assigned to one or two schools and serve all first-, second-, and third-year teachers in those schools by spanning the range of subject areas, from math and science to art and physical education. Using the platform of professional teaching standards, mentors focus their support and assistance on issues of pedagogy as they simultaneously seek out and draw on content-specific resources among their fellow mentors and the accomplished veteran teachers at the school sites. Fully aware of the potential challenge of this approach, the Durham program director fostered the sharing of resources and content knowledge throughout the mentor community.

In spite of the challenges that arise in a program that is not based on content matches, the program has experienced a number of gains. First, when mentors are deployed to a limited number of school sites, they get a much better sense of each school's culture.[2] Mentors develop stronger connections between their own strategies for moving practice forward and the strategies used within the school. Second, the approach supports relationship building between mentors and principals. Mentors report that simply being there—showing up regularly to support efforts of teachers in the building—allows them to be seen as a part of the school team and helps reassure principals that their interests and efforts are aligned. In some places, it also helps to initiate a tag-team approach. Mentors check in regularly with principals to ensure that they are following up on principals' concerns or areas of focus and can align their support with the site's supervision and evaluation process and time lines.

Other benefits accrue when mentors work outside their subject-matter or grade-level expertise. When mentors are exceptionally skilled and thoughtful, they are less likely to resort to "mentoring by telling" (the just-do-as-I-did model) and are more likely to become inquirers into practice alongside their novice colleagues. Like the new teachers, such mentors must seek out resources, reach out to colleagues, and gather data to help guide the novice's decision making and next instructional steps. Rather than diminish the expertise and knowledge of the mentor, this approach can provide a powerful model of mentor as lifelong learner and point out to the newly minted teacher that she is embarking on a professional journey of ongoing inquiry. This is a powerful model indeed, and it clearly works in Durham public schools.

This generalist approach is not necessarily appropriate for all programs. In Durham its success depends largely on the ability to identify mentors and leaders who are not only exceptionally skilled in moving instructional practice forward (a large enough task in itself) but also committed and able to reach beyond their own knowledge at a rapid pace. These individuals feel comfortable building the plane while flying it and are sufficiently proactive in identifying resources to ensure that they attain the content-focused tools to do so.

What types of programs might benefit from this approach? Does the specific context of Durham's program allow it to transcend the need for content-based matching? Would other programs be able to find mentors who have the unique skills to pull off this intensive, collaborative work? What are the implications for the research that suggests that content-based matches have a more profound impact on teacher and student outcomes?

NTC does not yet have the answers to these questions but looks forward to learning from other districts that build on some of this work to help improve our collective understanding.

Working conditions of beginning teachers

Some observers have described the sink-or-swim new teacher experience as a form of hazing. It goes somewhat like this: the newest teachers get the hardest-to-serve students—even though these teachers may be the least skilled; are assigned classes outside their grade or subject area of expertise—and they may be required to gain certification within a year; are enlisted to take on extra duties—ones that veteran teachers have earned the right to decline; and may find their classrooms devoid of resources—because those have been raided over the summer by their colleagues. In many places, this treatment may be thought of as a rite of passage and may be accompanied by a rather callous sentiment: "If I had to go through it . . ." or, "Well, we survived!"

Although well-designed, broadly endorsed mentoring programs can mitigate these factors, even the most effective program cannot overcome some of the negative working conditions new teachers must endure. Generally, principals who are worried about staffing classrooms don't want to deal with contract issues regarding seniority or tell veteran staff that after all their years of service they are losing their right to work with the "brighter" or more motivated students. Without external drivers, colleagues who endured the hazing rituals themselves are not inclined to break the pattern.

Our case study sites address this issue primarily by focusing on the role of the principal in creating conditions where new teachers thrive. Chicago incorporates a focus on support for new teachers within its evolving principal development program. This approach involves a collaboration between the CNTC's principal coaches, who work with new principals in many areas, and local area-based professional development for principals. Durham mentors are piloting and facilitating activities that use data from the state's Teacher Working Conditions survey to open up meaningful, site-based conversations focused on the conditions that will help new teachers succeed.[3] Boston is creating toolkits and professional development training on the topic and asks mentors to engage in informative discussions to teach principals how to be more effective in supporting new teachers. New York has developed a school review process that seeks to unpack the conditions of the school and better understand the ways in which teachers are and are not being supported.

These approaches, while promising, present two major challenges. First, they focus on the principal as the sole agent of change. Although teachers' working conditions vary within a district from site to site, principals are not the sole decision makers about many factors and policies affecting the lives of new teachers. Everything from how new teachers are recruited, interviewed, hired, assigned to a school, and given a grade-level or subject-matter assignment may be predicated on strongly held traditions, norms, policies, and contractual agreements that may extend beyond a single principal's ability to influence or transcend. Indeed, school leaders can affect changes in site policies, norms, attitudes, and practices, and they can become advocates alongside their mentors for the resources and district-level policies that will improve the working conditions of new teachers and thereby the learning conditions of those teachers' students. But the larger system has a significant, and perhaps even greater, responsibility to set the expectations and conditions that support these changes.

Second, in some cases efforts to support changes in the working conditions (also described as teaching and learning conditions) for new teachers are led primarily by mentors or program leaders. This arrangement is problematic because mentors and program leaders need to have as their central focus the acceleration of each new teacher's classroom practice. Certainly, teaching and learning conditions in a school are a significant factor in whether or not a teacher is successful, and mentors are responsible for advocating for their beginning teachers' rights and access to fair working conditions. But short- and long-term outcomes need to be balanced by program leaders and mentors as they set priorities and allocate their resources and time. The work of improving working conditions for new teachers should be shared by a number of stakeholder groups: teachers associations, principals, district office leaders, veteran teachers, and community members (especially when new teachers in some neighborhoods can barely afford to pay local rents). The desired outcome is clear, but the solution is much more complex.

To see success, school district leaders need to identify the best strategies for creating change in schools that lead to better teaching and learning conditions for all teachers. Program leaders may determine that mentors who work across the system, especially when well selected and widely respected, may have a role in supporting this work. However, NTC has yet to define fully what this role looks like and determine what additional structures and investments are necessary to realize true success.

Aligning support for new teachers

What does it mean to align initiatives, and what does it look like? The mentoring programs in our cases have approached alignment with two purposes: (1) to synchronize and enhance each teacher's mentoring experience and (2) to build synergy and strengthen the impact of teacher development efforts throughout the system. The first purpose focuses on the individual new teacher, and the second looks at the experiences of all teachers. Both are complex endeavors that require collaboration, transparency, and forethought and can challenge even the most effective programs.

Most school districts have an array of initiatives that focuses on issues of teacher effectiveness and instructional practice, but often there is limited coordination of these efforts and among the people involved. Curriculum coaches, mentors, assistant principals, university supervisors, department chairs, specialists, professional developers, and others bring a variety of ideas, tools, and resources to the table—each with different goals, frameworks, and expectations. New teachers, especially, feel this disconnect and often report feeling inundated and confused by competing visions and the sheer quantity of expectations placed on them. The irony, of course, is that new teachers, who have historically been ignored or undersupported, are now, in some districts, the overwhelmed beneficiaries of too much support. As long as the support is idiosyncratic, with little coordination or alignment among initiatives, new teachers cannot fully benefit from this abundance of riches.

Because of the structure of the model in Durham, mentors have had time to develop relationships with school staff. In fact, because the system uses a generalist approach, mentors have been encouraged to reach out to other teachers to support their subject-matter knowledge and understanding of curriculum implementation. This policy has encouraged strategic cooperation between various support providers and, where appropriate, has enabled mentors to share knowledge of the mentoring tools and strategies they use. Some mentors have begun opening up the work they are doing with new teachers to other educators in the school by facilitating professional development and participating in or supporting professional learning communities on-site. The result is stronger and more strategic links across the many instructional initiatives that touch the classroom.

In Chicago, there has been an extensive and concerted outreach to the leaders responsible for overseeing professional development and the principals in each area.[4] The Chicago NTC (CNTC) uses a three-pronged approach that links mentoring, literacy, and principal development. Program leaders work to ensure that all messages clearly articulate the alignment of these professional development efforts and help school leaders understand the district priorities for supporting instructional growth. To align the support strategies throughout the system, Chicago Public Schools has also worked with CNTC to train all literacy coaches in a subset of mentoring protocols and tools used with the new teachers.

Boston leaders foster alignment through regular conversations with all major stakeholders involved in supporting new teachers. With the assistance of a local foundation, high-level representatives from the mentoring program, the Boston Teacher Residency Program, the Office of Human Resources, the Office of Teaching and Learning, the Office of Instructional Technology, and the Boston Plan for Excellence (a research-based local education fund) have been meeting from the start of the program to coordinate and promote one another's efforts and to build a common vision for support of new teachers at the district and school levels. The group uses data from the Boston Plan for Excellence to identify outcomes and challenges and to consider program improvements. Mentors from both the mentoring program and the Boston Teacher Residency Program also attend joint training whenever possible and share data about new teacher practice.

All of these strategies were useful, but mentors and program leaders from all case study sites suggest that the results of alignment efforts are far from systematic and are idiosyncratic at best. For example, when mentors sought to collaborate with others who were also supporting new teachers, they were successful only when the other staff members were open and prioritized the time to collaborate. This had more to do with the personality types—and the relationships between mentors and other staffers—than with the protocols calling for collaboration.

If new (and perhaps all) teachers are to benefit from a coherent approach to the advancement of their instructional practice, then programs need to examine integrated and aligned structures that allow for systematic and authentic collaboration at every level.

This may be a tall order for large urban school districts that consist of myriad departments and offices focusing on different initiatives—especially where departments are accustomed to working in isolation. The programs described here have begun to explore strategies that move them from a place of isolation to alignment and collaboration. However, to transform this powerful systemic trend (with strong historical precedent), districts will continue to grapple with the question of how to create sustainable structures that support true collaboration, based on an aligned vision for instructional progress, at both the school and the district level.

Sanctioning time for interaction between mentors and beginning teachers

A recent study on the NYC induction program indicates that time for interactions between a mentor and new teacher can impact student achievement.[5] When teachers receive less than one hour of mentoring assistance per week, there is no evidence that mentoring has any impact on student achievement. When teachers meet for what the NTC considers a bare minimum of one hour per week, at least one major study shows gains by students in reading and math. These results point to a fundamental and self-evident consideration for mentoring programs: mentors must have adequate, sanctioned time to mentor.

The NTC has long recommended 1.5 to 2.5 hours per week of interaction time between a mentor and each beginning teacher. Based on more than twenty years of implementing its model, the NTC has seen this as a balance point between resource allocation and impact. However, many urban districts struggle to meet these time allocations.

New York City mentors struggled to meet this time target for two reasons: (1) a caseload of seventeen or more new teachers and (2) the travel demands of serving new teachers in as many as six or more schools.[6] Given the challenges of traveling from one school site to another in an urban setting where parking is challenging and public transportation is the only viable alternative, mentors often find their time with new teachers significantly reduced.

Chicago struggles with similar issues, because it has a mentor-to-teacher ratio of 1:16 and mentors often need to visit a high number of schools. Transportation between schools may be somewhat less complex than in New York but nonetheless is time consuming. For this reason, program leaders differentiate caseloads for special education mentors and reduce the number of new teachers they serve to twelve so that new special education teachers can benefit from these mentors' expertise.

In Durham, mentor-to-new-teacher ratios may not be the best indicator of whether teachers are receiving the appropriate amount of time with their mentors. Because DPS mentors work with all new teachers in a given school, program leadership, in consultation with the mentors, occasionally allows caseloads to grow beyond the recommended ratios to avoid having to assign another mentor to a site. The determining factor rests upon giving mentors the fewest number of schools, thereby reducing overall travel time and increasing a mentor's time to interact with school-based personnel.

In all these cases, however, new questions have emerged that have called into question our understanding of how to think about, and allocate, a mentor's time. In their efforts to build relationships with principals and school staff and to learn from or push school learning communities to support instructional progress, mentors (especially those who work in a large number of schools) sometimes have difficulty finding sufficient time to meet with each of their new teachers.

This raises interesting questions. How do mentors learn to draw the line with regard to helping with general teacher development initiatives at the sites where they are based? And where is that line? Mentors can have a powerful skill set focused on moving instructional practice forward. But should they be the ones charged with facilitating small school learning teams or supporting principals in transforming teaching and learning conditions? If so, how does that impact the time they spend with their new teachers? How do districts adjust mentor-to-teacher ratios to compensate for lost time? What is the optimum school caseload? And where is the balance point between the number of schools and subject-matter or grade-level matches?

These questions continue to play out in various district contexts. They likely must be answered, in the short term, by program leaders who are willing to try various models and strategies that address the critical issue of time and are flexible and responsive to what works. In the long term, the hope is that through trial and error, knowledge sharing, and a commitment to excellence, those who work on these issues will eventually agree on the right answers.

LEVERAGE POINTS FOR CHANGE

One of the most salient truths underlying all aspects of new teacher development is that there is a large gap between theory and practice. Just because a teacher has knowledge of best practices does not mean he understands how to apply that knowledge to his everyday routines in the classroom. By the same token, the promising practices (and deepening questions) described in this chapter provide some general knowledge about how to explore and support efforts that lead to meaningful change. This next section seeks to provide potential entry points that will allow education leaders across the board to apply this knowledge in creative and substantive ways. Some of these entry points require a new vision of the school system as we know it, and others encourage small tweaks in current programs that would have a potentially profound impact. All these entry points lead us toward creating a common vision, shared ownership, and mutual respect for efforts that lead to better outcomes for students and educators.

State policy

In each case study, states laid the foundation for the important work of mentoring. In Durham, the state required that all first-, second-, and third-year teachers receive support and recommended full-time release programs. In Illinois, officials developed high-quality mentoring program standards and funded an initiative that allows districts to apply for funding to support effective programs on the ground. New York State and Massachusetts modified their certification requirements to require all new teachers to receive mentoring before receiving a credential, and New York reestablished a grant program to districts wanting to implement high-quality mentoring programs.

Although the funding in each of these states has not been sufficient to cover the total costs of full-time release programs, the state contexts supported conditions that allowed these programs to emerge. By underscoring research and articulating messages about the need for new teacher support and attaching legislation that moved the education system in some ways, these leaders created an entry point for school districts to have the conversation about high-quality mentoring. The seed money provided in some states helped leverage innovative dialogues into significant change.

Many other states—including Alabama, Alaska, Connecticut, Idaho, Hawaii, Oregon, Ohio, and Texas—are revising (or have recently revised) their state programs to include high-quality standards for mentoring. Their success will not be based on the size or scope of the state program but rather on their ability to create, support, and sustain high-quality mentoring programs statewide, especially in the urban settings that are most in need of support. In addition to high-quality state program standards, states need to develop infrastructure support and to model best practices so that district knowledge can expand and program implementation can be successful over time.

Teacher unions and associations

The early and ongoing engagement of teacher unions and associations is critical to ensure the success of comprehensive mentoring programs. Importantly, new teacher mentoring also represents an essential strategy for teacher unions to meet their own goals.

At the local, state, and federal levels, teacher unions and associations are in transition. They are trying to pave a path toward a new type of organization—one that recognizes and prioritizes traditional union values such as salary, benefits, and working conditions while also supporting the progress of educational issues that impact and improve student outcomes. This effort is a challenge for many local leaders seeking to serve those educators (traditionally veteran educators) who see the union's primary role as protecting teacher rights. At the same time, unions need the active interest and participation of a new wave of teachers who are interested in having a significant voice in reforming schools so that all students have the opportunity to learn.

Teacher mentoring represents one of the few crossover issues that intersects the two ideologies. If the attrition of new teachers is to be addressed, unions must prioritize advocacy for better new teacher working conditions *and* development of new teacher effectiveness in providing instruction. Unions historically have been effective advocates in supporting better working conditions in schools and are emerging as influential voices in supporting instructional improvement. The Boston and New York City examples show how district leaders and instruction-focused union leaders can pair up to lead an initiative that prioritizes both.

Engaging unions early in the process of design, development, and oversight of mentoring programs is a win-win situation for districts and local teacher associations. It helps both parties meet identified goals, and it provides opportunities for collaboration that potentially can strengthen relationships and support cooperation in the important work of developing a competent, caring, and professional teacher workforce.

Collaborative, rigorous communities of practice

Within the past several years an interest has emerged in what many call professional learning communities (PLCs) in schools. Unfortunately, the term has been so overused that its meaning perhaps has been diluted. Many people don't understand what such communities look like on the ground or how to apply the concepts to schools and classrooms.

The NTC's model of effective professional development is grounded in PLCs—or, more specifically, communities of practice—that infuse rigorous conversation about instruction and use data, inquiry, and structured protocols to drive those discussions toward improved learning for mentors, teachers and students. When these conversations are recursive, responsive, and ongoing, they can be profound leverage points for helping educators apply their knowledge and skills in meaningful ways.

Although the role of the mentor historically has been to support teachers through one-on-one interactions, many mentors are leading the development of robust communities of practice. In Chicago, mentors and program leaders facilitate collaborative conversations about literacy to support teachers in learning more deeply how to help students learn how to read and write. In Durham, mentors are explicitly asked to sit in on, support, and in some cases lead the PLC efforts at the school level. In New York, former mentors seek to prompt schoolwide conversations about teaching standards and develop other tools that support instructional growth. In Boston, mentors facilitate new teacher seminars and support principals in establishing collaborative communities of practice.

Mentors who have been trained in the NTC model are natural leaders for this work. They have exceptional knowledge about assessing and moving teacher practice forward. They have highly developed skills in working with other adult learners. Perhaps most important, they have experienced robust learning communities that prioritize rigor, professionalism, and results. Yet district leaders need to recognize certain critical elements before they can capitalize on this potential entry point.

First, not all mentors are effective facilitators of schoolwide groups and processes. Working with adults one-on-one calls on a different skill set than does working with groups of educators and school leadership teams. It is vital to give mentors the skills and knowledge to understand the intricacies of group facilitation and school-level change to help them navigate the jump from one-on-one support to school-level change—especially when mentors seek to work with school leaders to develop collaborative teams. District and program leaders should first identify mentors who have an aptitude for working at both the school level and the classroom level, and provide ongoing training and coaching around this work, before pushing this type of agenda.

Second, when mentors are required to support or lead schoolwide reform efforts, it necessarily diminishes the amount of time for one-on-one coaching of new teachers. Because time for interactions is one of the key components of instructional mentoring—and the one that research shows has most impact on student outcomes—the benefit to new teachers can be diluted (or negated) when mentors are spread too thin.

The NTC proposes two possibilities for addressing this gap. First, districts can reduce mentors' caseloads, especially for those who are proving to have capacity in this area. Second, if mentors have a role, and training, in supporting PLCs after their mentor rotation is complete, then their ability to push schools forward in developing robust communities of practice can be catapulted. This approach requires a human capital strategy that gives mentors a school leadership or school change role once they leave the role of mentor.

Professional learning communities will have limited impact if the results of these conversations do not reach the classroom. In other words, teachers learn best when the information can be applied directly to their classroom contexts. Talking about instruction can be positive in grade-level, cross-division, or other collaborative teams, but often new teachers are not sure how to apply the information to their own teaching strategies. Having mentors or other trained educators visit, collect data, and collaboratively discuss what is actually happening in the classrooms of new teachers are essential parts of a successful movement of new teacher practice.

If such mentoring strategies can be tied to PLCs (for example, if mentors and new teachers participate together in grade-level teams), then the impact of the work with new teachers can be enhanced, and other teachers in the community can benefit from shared learning. Such a strategy must be carefully crafted to ensure that confidentiality agreements are not breached, but this idea might be explored as districts consider how to magnify the impact of their PLC and mentoring initiatives.

Principal training and certification programs

One of the most important challenges of mentoring programs is how little school leaders know about new teacher development. Principal training and certification programs usually provide limited (if any) information about the needs of new teachers and the importance of their development in making an impact on student outcomes.

Without a nuanced understanding of new teacher development, many principals perpetuate poor working conditions for new teachers, set unrealistically high expectations for instruction and student outcomes, and do not provide the support necessary to help new teachers achieve success. These shortcomings not only add to teacher frustration and exacerbate rates of attrition but also foster ineffective teaching practices in new teachers' classrooms.

Mentors and district leaders seek to address this gap in knowledge through on-the-job knowledge sharing. However, because of the many competing priorities of principals, these efforts are only partially effective. The educational community must engage principals in this important conversation much earlier than they typically do. Asking that principal training and certification programs include support for new teachers as a critical element can be a significant leverage point for increasing the knowledge of school leaders at scale and for subverting many of the structures that obstruct new teacher success from the beginning.

University schools of education

A recent controversial report by the former president of Teachers College has called on universities to engage in significant and serious reforms to make their schools of education more responsive to educator and school needs.[7] Although this report has been a powerful motivator for change, the call for reform is not new. Educational advocates have been calling for universities to bridge the gap between theory and practice, and develop stronger connections with public schools, for many years. Yet many universities have not answered these calls, because they haven't had the vehicles for making change a reality. Generally, creating strong partnerships with public school entities is not seen as an academic exercise, and little precedent has been set that shows where and how universities and public schools can collaborate effectively to improve instructional practice.

More recently, a number of schools of education are breaking new ground in partnering with school districts. Many of these institutions use mentoring as their primary entry point for developing connections. They see mentoring programs as the link between pre-service and accomplished teaching. As a result, they have begun to identify, create, facilitate, support, and advocate programs that help teacher candidates and recent teacher graduates draw connections between theory and practice. Information gleaned from these efforts helps inform, and in some places transform, the curriculum and pedagogy used in universities to support teacher candidate success.

These efforts provide promising indicators that schools of education have the potential to become more responsive to district needs and may be able to serve as catalysts for developing high-quality mentoring programs.

MOVING FORWARD

The emerging trends discussed in this chapter seek to support school district and other educational leaders in understanding critical nuances of implementing high-quality mentoring. By highlighting questions that persist across settings and by visiting some of the strategies invoked to address challenges in the work, NTC hopes to provide readers, especially district leaders, with a leg up on creating meaningful and sustainable change that leads to new teacher success.

Some of these ideas, however, represent new thinking for NTC, and new ways of thinking about the work in general. Readers should not consider these scenarios as a foolproof plan for implementing high-quality mentoring. On the contrary, readers should consider these efforts and ideas part of a critical dialogue that seeks to inform and build innovative strategies that lead to better outcomes for teachers and students. NTC does not yet have all the answers. Hopefully these insights will continue to allow us to dig deeper and will help us identify some of the right questions.

Still, having a minimum base of knowledge of how to move forward in districts based on lessons learned can be a powerful platform for success. With this in mind, we move to chapter 9, which encapsulates what NTC has learned and provides concrete recommendations for educational stakeholders who are interested in furthering the cause.

9
—

Implications and Recommendations
for Educational Stakeholders

Chapter 8 explores the trends, questions, and levers for change, looking specifically across the four NTC case studies presented in this book. This chapter examines the implications based on some of the most policy-friendly lessons learned in chapter 8, while drawing on NTC's two decades of experience in the field, to provide powerful recommendations to readers interested in building on the work. The recommendations are tailored to specific audiences and aim to support school district leaders, program directors, researchers, universities, philanthropists, union officers, community leaders, and other educational advocates as they connect the knowledge NTC has developed to real change that matters for kids.

IMPLICATIONS FOR LEADERS IN URBAN SCHOOL SYSTEMS

Leaders in urban school systems represent the linchpin of NTC's efforts to transform teaching and learning in the United States. Their active involvement in the design and oversight of programs will determine to what extent programs will have the capacity to succeed. NTC is still developing knowledge about what it takes to create all the conditions for success—and what that success looks like—but it has developed at least some basic recommendations that may help leaders help their mentoring programs, and ultimately the teachers and students of new teachers, thrive.

Do mentoring only if you can do it right

High-quality mentoring can be a powerful strategy for transforming and supporting educational excellence. When done well, it can greatly reduce new teacher attrition, improve new teacher effectiveness, provide a cost savings to schools, and build human capital in urban settings. However, when programs are not aligned with the key principles of effective mentoring, or when programs are not implemented fully, such outcomes are not realized and critical dollars are all but wasted.

District leaders interested in creating or improving programs should closely review the principles of high-quality mentoring (outlined in chapter 2) and take time with all key instructional leaders in the system to explore how the district might interpret and apply the principles within its specific setting. Additionally, leaders will have a greater chance of success when they work closely with staff to identify innovative strategies to ensure full implementation in spite of any operational, programmatic, and political obstacles that may impede efforts.

Although it is important to ensure that all elements of a program be implemented with fidelity, a particular focus on the following principles may help districts realize the most positive outcomes:

- Rigorous mentor recruitment and selection
- Intensive and ongoing professional development for mentors
- Sanctioned time for mentor–teacher interactions (1.5–2.5 hours per week)
- Structures that support regular engagement of school leaders, school staff, and key district stakeholders

Carefully identify program leaders, and give them needed resources

High-quality mentoring programs are complex efforts that demand exceptional leadership if they are to succeed at all levels. Such leaders are not necessarily easy to find. They represent educators with an expansive and unique skill set that isn't always prioritized in school settings. The following descriptors represent the most updated thinking on the qualities of an effective mentor program leader. Before developing a program, district leaders should consider engaging in a rigorous selection process to recruit instructional leaders in the system who have a strong track record for the following:

- Excellence in teaching
- Moving teacher practice forward
- Understanding and advocating for the needs of new teachers
- Creating professional, data-driven, and results-oriented communities of practice
- Tailoring professional development to meet the specific needs of teachers
- Navigating schoolwide and districtwide priorities
- Generating and disseminating effective communication strategies
- Managing complex operations
- Empowering educators to develop and pursue their own vision for excellence in education

Once hired, mentor program leaders need the conditions that will allow them to capitalize on their robust skill set. It is always recommended that mentor program leaders be hired full time and, where funding allows, provided with secondary support personnel (assistant directors, mentor leadership positions, and administrative support) to engage in the time-intensive, multifaceted work of instructional transformation.

Recruit and select the best mentors

Recruitment and selection of mentors are possibly the most important variables in the success or failure of a mentor program. Yet there are myriad obstacles in urban systems to finding the right people to be mentors. There are also myriad creative and strategic opportunities to surmount these obstacles and find mentors who truly have the vision, talent, and competence needed to transform teaching and learning in schools.

To be successful, district and program leaders need to commit to raising the level of visibility and cachet of the program from the onset and need to insist on the highest possible standards for recruitment and selection. Programs must aggressively reach out to find a subset of the most talented teachers in the system, something that is not always an easy task. Programs might consider using evidence of high student achievement gains with diverse populations as a criterion for selection and explicitly reaching out to high achievers such as teachers of the year or National Board certified teachers. Programs also should develop personal outreach strategies to those they know are outstanding teachers or other methods that help isolate and recruit the crème de la crème of educators throughout the system.

However, it is important to remember that not all great teachers make great mentors. These outstanding educators must also possess the disposition of excellent mentors (having exceptional interpersonal skills, being lifelong learners, having the respect of peers, having a history of advocacy, etc.). When combined, these attributes are powerful resources for supporting and transforming instruction in classroom and school settings.

To achieve success in these endeavors, it is critical to start the recruitment and selection process early (well before top educators commit to teaching or other job offers) and to provide sufficient time to identify, recruit, follow up on, and select mentors. Senior district leaders will see greatest success when they personally participate in selection, especially in the early stages, to flag to all members of the district that new teacher mentors are highly valued members of the community. It is also critical to ensure that those who are responsible for ultimately selecting mentors use rigorous standards (focusing on the attributes of effective mentors) and are knowledgeable about instruction, adult learning, and, where possible, instructionally intensive mentoring.

Ensure that teachers and mentors have sufficient time for interacting

Emerging evidence suggests that full-time release for mentors may have a more powerful impact than part-time and no-release-time models.[1] Yet even full-time release programs can (unintentionally) provide insufficient time between mentors and new teachers, and that leads to diluted or negated instructional progress and retention.

Regardless of the type of model used or the structure in which it is housed, districts must develop systems that ensure that new teachers receive the minimum time necessary to move practice forward. The New Teacher Center recommends 1.5–2.5 hours per week. Capping full-time release models to 15:1 teacher-to-mentor ratios (or lower in hard-to-staff schools) and limiting the number of schools served by mentors (ideally to no more than four) can help districts reach these time targets. If mentors are expected to take on additional duties (e.g., provide professional development, facilitate school collaborative teams), their caseloads should be reduced proportionally so that new teachers do not get shortchanged and do have every opportunity to succeed.

Integrate teaching standards and formative assessment of teacher growth

Professional teaching standards, the NTC Continuum of Teacher Development, and formative assessment protocols can be powerful tools for developing a common language and vision for moving instruction forward. These tools provide a useful platform for change between new teachers and mentors. However, if only mentors and teachers use this language, it will have a lesser impact than if all educators are fluent.

Thoughtful dissemination and training strategies are needed so that educators throughout the system understand how to use these tools in ways that support the application of knowledge and skills in the classroom. District and program leaders might consider creating mentor leadership roles that push systems integration of this knowledge (especially after candidates leave the role of mentor). Districts that focus on implementing professional learning communities might especially consider the role of mentor leaders in informing, shaping, and leading the efforts and provide the professional training and support to ensure they can be successful.

When accompanied by significant support and training in how to use these tools to support teacher development (as opposed to accountability alone), teaching standards can be embedded in school evaluation protocols, tenure decisions, and other districtwide structures that can serve as levers for systemic change.

Build awareness, interest, and engagement of principals

Most principals receive limited information on the needs of new teachers, either in principal credentialing programs or on the job. Many are not aware of the role that support for new teachers can play in realizing principals' goals of school excellence, or they are not sure how to focus their school's new teacher development efforts. District leaders are in a strategic position to develop structures that help administrators better understand the importance of new teacher development and identify the most promising strategies for supporting the success of their new teachers. To achieve success, programs and districts should prioritize a twofold effort that encourages principals to (1) engage with and support mentors in improving new teacher practice and (2) work with teachers, school leadership teams, union representatives, and other stakeholders to create the working conditions necessary for new teachers to thrive.

Where mentors are of exceptional caliber, district leaders might consider adopting the generalist approach, whereby mentors work with new teachers in only one or two schools, allowing mentors to develop strong relationships with principals and school communities. District leaders should be aware, though, that in these models it is important to ensure that programs have specific structures set up to share and build mentor content knowledge in a fast-paced environment.

Some district leaders may seek to build in a program component focused exclusively on principal support, giving them the tools they need to prioritize and become expert in developing teacher practice. Other leaders may engage in intensive, multifaceted outreach strategies to build relationships with principals individually and across the system. Ensuring that messages are always tailored to meet the needs of site-based leaders engenders increased ownership by principals and stronger application of ideas into action.

Districts are also encouraged to explore new strategies to improve engagement of principals in the important work of supporting new teachers.

Coordinate staff, communication, and alignment of initiatives

Most urban school districts are not set up to communicate effectively or align efforts across settings. As a result, the support new teachers receive can be disconnected and disjointed, sometimes exacerbating attrition and stifling instructional progress. To avoid this significant, and increasingly common, obstacle to support, district leaders might explore structures that allow for deep and lasting cross-division and cross-initiative collaboration. Such efforts should seek to ensure that all communication about or from instructional initiatives helps get everyone in the system on the same page about what effective instruction looks like—and how to implement that understanding of effective instruction within every classroom.

There may be perceptions that there is not enough time and resources to achieve such a high level of coordination. However, the alternative is to significantly dilute the potential impact of initiatives that touch the lives of new (and all) teachers.

Capitalize on the strengths of key stakeholders

Teacher unions, teacher associations, and universities can be powerful potential allies in the work of mentoring. They not only support deeper and more meaningful implementation of programs but also serve as key leaders in the work, advocacy partners, and gatekeepers to sustainability of programs. To ensure that their insights, ownership, and political leverage are incorporated into the design and rollout of the program and are included as it grows and deepens, district and program leaders should invite these parties to the table at the earliest stages of development. Anticipate that there may be differences that arise in the vision, time line, and implementation of the program, and have the resilience and wisdom to prioritize strong relationships over all else. (This does not mean conceding on important points, but respecting and valuing each other's perspectives as you seek to come up with solutions.) Remember that no collaboration is easy, and have confidence that outcomes are stronger and longer lasting when the political will for change is aligned and owned across multiple layers of the system.

Intensify support in hard-to-staff and low-performing schools

New teachers in low-performing and hard-to-staff schools have a steeper learning curve than those who teach in higher-functioning schools. They generally endure more-challenging working conditions and have less access to meaningful instructional support. In some cases this is the result of toxic school environments that offer limited opportunities for deep collaboration and support. In other cases, schools simply don't have capacity, because high levels of turnover deplete human resources and leave few experienced educators to provide effective instructional support. Additional time for mentoring interactions, higher levels of advocacy for addressing instructional needs, and facilitated observations with veteran teachers in other schools will significantly help new teachers succeed in these environments. This may mean a significantly lower caseload for mentors working in such communities, empowering mentors with school-level data to support improved teaching and learning conditions, and identifying other creative strategies for fostering conditions that will help new (and all) teachers succeed.

IMPLICATIONS FOR STATE AND FEDERAL POLICY MAKERS

A number of legislative efforts are currently under way to support new teachers, but mandating mentor programs is not sufficient. Programs must be high quality, instructionally intensive, and implemented fully (in ways that are aligned with policies!) if we want to see better outcomes for teachers and kids. Funding traditional, nonrigorous programs might as well be thought of as throwing money—taxpayers' money—away. Policy makers are in a unique period of time to take advantage of the entry points available to build knowledge *and infrastructure* that support fully realized and effective programs at scale.

Build on momentum, especially in disadvantaged districts

The four states where the case studies for this book were situated, along with nearly a dozen other states and the federal government, have been actively engaged in efforts to build more effective mentoring policies. In many cases, these activities have set the stage for allowing districts to transform their induction and mentoring programs. The provision of incentives, funding, and sometimes knowledge of best practices alone has served as the catalyst that has led many districts to action.

For the past several years, states and federal agencies have sought to build awareness that teacher mentoring—when comprehensive, instructionally intensive, and high quality—can significantly improve new teacher retention and effectiveness, enhance student achievement, deliver significant cost savings to school districts, and serve as a critical lever for reducing the student achievement gap. These agencies have built this awareness through various strategies, including developing high-quality state mentoring program standards; requiring mentoring of new teachers before certification;

initiating pilot programs to model best practices; funding statewide full-time release models; connecting mentoring to professional development standards and teacher leadership opportunities; creating statewide learning networks; and many more. These efforts are beginning to bear fruit, with hundreds of districts around the country thinking differently about the way they support new teachers.

Policy makers must take advantage of this moment to capitalize on the knowledge and momentum that are building for the power of mentoring programs to transform the teaching profession and provide equitable outcomes for students. It represents a politically easy win, because high-quality teacher mentoring is one of the most politically amenable strategies in school reform. It is championed by district leaders, teacher unions, universities, community groups, alternative certification programs, Democrats, Republicans, and many other constituencies typically on opposing sides. It is a strategy that transcends political partisanship. But even though teacher mentoring can greatly reduce the student achievement gap and improve teacher quality in all schools, only policy makers can ensure that comprehensive, instructionally intensive programs are accessible at scale around the United States—and especially in the high-poverty, high-minority systems that are most in need of such support.

Invest in infrastructure

While states and the U.S. government are spearheading efforts to support new teacher success, the reality is that districts themselves are responsible for implementing the vision. Where districts have the capacity to succeed, there may be some powerful gains made. However, not all districts have the knowledge, skills, or funding to make such visions a reality.

State and federal institutions interested in supporting excellent programs at scale will need to invest in building the infrastructure necessary to ensure that districts have the tools they need to succeed. In most cases—yes—this means that funding is needed. However, it goes beyond funding. It means the development of preassessments and the provision of technical assistance to ensure that districts have the basic elements in place before they begin to engage in reform. It means the creation of cross-district learning networks driven by data so that district programs can reflect on and learn from one another and can see themselves progressing through a cycle of continual improvement. It means creating regional or statewide evaluations so that states can be fully informed about the levels of implementation of state policy and can seek to use this data to support (rather than punish) programs that need improvement. It absolutely requires the regular collection and analysis of impact data to justify and sustain the program within the region and to ensure that all incoming policy makers are aware of the power of the work to transform schools.

When policy changes are coupled with sufficient funding and infrastructure, then new teachers in the entire region—and their students—will have the opportunity to thrive.

IMPLICATIONS FOR RESEARCHERS

This book lays out several pieces of the known research on mentoring. This research is still in its nascent stages and does not yet represent a rigorous body of evidence that yields full understanding of the impact of mentoring and the qualities of mentoring that matter most. NTC has developed a framework for understanding how to develop and implement programs, but researchers hold the key to drawing conclusive links to impact. Independent researchers can contribute significantly to the education community at large by replicating and validating (or challenging) the studies articulated in this book and by answering questions that continue to perplex the field.

Undertake rigorous research

The research on mentoring and induction is too young and too thin to claim any causal relationships or make any conclusive statements. With the potential significant expansion of policies to support new teachers, the need to support rigorous studies in the field has become urgent. Researchers who have the capacity to look closely at the impact of fully implemented, high-quality mentor programs should seek to make such research a top priority.

In addition to looking at the impact of programs as a summative assessment, however, it is critical to build the skills and knowledge of those who are implementing programs, so that they can seek to create the most effective conditions for success in their settings. Such research might be seen as formative assessment data that can guide district, state, and federal leaders in the allocation of resources so that the greatest numbers of students can benefit.

To achieve this end, researchers might consider studies that help unpack the black box of mentoring. Specifically, researchers might consider researching the following questions:

- Which components of high-quality mentoring are the most highly correlated with student achievement gains and teacher retention in high-intensity programs?

- How important is subject-matter matching of teachers and mentors?

- Is there a specific set of selection criteria that yields effective mentors?

- Does the quality of mentors improve as a program matures, and can programs shorten this time?

- What are the most important components of mentor training?

- How does collaboration between mentors, administrators, and site-based staff impact teacher learning outcomes?

- How do working conditions (reduced workload, better teaching assignments) affect teacher growth when paired with high-intensity mentoring?

- Would pairing mentors with principals make mentoring more effective?

- Are three-year rotations for mentors beneficial for districts, or should districts hold on to mentors longer?

- What is the maximum number of schools that a mentor can successfully work in?

IMPLICATIONS FOR PHILANTHROPISTS, ADVOCATES, PRACTITIONERS, AND OTHERS

We are at an important moment. Mentoring can serve as key strategic leverage for improving the teaching profession and equalizing outcomes for poor and underserved youth. But it also has the potential to become the next "reform du jour" that is forsaken as the pendulum swings to another topic. The outcome relies not on the ability to mandate mentoring programs but on the ability of our community to understand, advocate for, implement, and sustain highly effective programs.

Build knowledge and understanding of mentoring

Although mentoring as a strategy for reform is growing in some circles, there is a far distance between where we are now and where we need to be if we are to impact the lives of all new teachers throughout the United States (and abroad). Parents, funders, educators, unions, nonprofits, media, universities, community groups, policy makers, for-profits, practitioners, and all people who affect, or are affected by, what happens in the public schools can come together to influence change when the need is compelling and messages are aligned.

As teacher mentoring emerges as one potential strategy to improve equity and excellence in our public schools and as the research becomes clearer, the need becomes more compelling and the mission more concrete: we must drive the message forward in ways that resonate with communities at every level, and we must build the political will to realize success in every context. This action requires resources, collaboration, persistence, patience, and an unyielding confidence that by giving all new teachers the chance to succeed, we will give all students the chance to succeed.

There are no mathematical formulas for getting these messages out or for supporting efforts that lead to more effective understanding. There are, however, some strategies that can be invoked to further this effort. For example, philanthropists interested in supporting the work of mentoring may consider the following funding strategies:

- Provide seed money to support programs in school districts while insisting that districts implement the components of high-quality mentoring.

- Provide modest gap funding that allows districts to implement some components they otherwise would not have been able to implement.

- Fund rigorous research that helps track the impact of mentoring programs and answer the research questions mentioned earlier.

- Provide funding that allows districts to intensify mentoring support in hard-to-staff and low-performing schools.

- Fund training for school leaders, instructional coaches and staff, and others in districts where mentors are being trained to ensure aligned support for new teachers.

- Fund meetings that bring together district leaders from multiple departments to discuss human capital strategies that address the needs of new teachers.

- Allow districts to apply innovations to current models and tools, especially those that address the ongoing challenges described in this book.

Practitioners can monitor the ability of districts to implement the components of high-quality induction with integrity and can talk to district leaders about the power of their work. Specifically, they can do the following:

- Engage researchers to study and evaluate program design and implementation, and advocate for program modifications and resources where necessary.

- Encourage cross-division conversations about the work of mentoring (and other strategies for moving instruction forward), and build on opportunities to improve collaboration and impact at the school and district level.

- Design a comprehensive oversight strategy that is supported by, and accountable to, representatives from all major stakeholders in the system.

- Explain the power of interactions between mentors and new teachers, telling the stories of teacher successes to educational stakeholders across the district.

Educational advocates and enthusiasts can seek to communicate the power of high-quality mentoring to those who can influence public and political support for change, including media, policy makers, community leaders, union advocates, and others. Primary points for advocacy should focus on the power of high-quality mentoring to:

- Improve new teacher retention
- Accelerate new teacher effectiveness
- Improve student outcomes (especially for the most underserved populations)

- Provide cost savings to districts
- Support a career ladder (which benefits teachers and students) by allowing master educators to take leadership roles outside school or district administration
- Reignite veteran teachers' passion for teaching and learning
- Serve as a foundation for human capital strategies that seek to help teachers develop and apply the skills and knowledge of effective teaching to their classroom

FINAL THOUGHTS

Educational leaders across the United States, and in many countries around the globe, are currently seeking out strategies that support new teachers. In recognition of the need to stem the high rates of attrition of new teachers and to give the students of new teachers a chance for success, practitioners, policy makers, and advocates are attempting to uncover the right path to ensure that new teachers have what they need to succeed.

The ideas presented here are neither comprehensive nor absolute. They represent what the New Teacher Center knows at one moment in time about practices and policies that foster, or inhibit, change that matters for new teachers and kids. Our greatest hope is that district leaders, and other educational change agents, will use these insights as a foundation that allows them to conceptualize and implement even stronger programs. In doing so, they no doubt will find new ways to innovate, answer persistent questions, resolve systemic challenges, find new questions to ask, discover new systemic challenges, and spread best practices that get us closer to our goal: an excellent education for all students.

In this endeavor, it is important to remember that it is not the absence of obstacles that defines our success. Rather, it is our courage to deeply understand, name, and lead toward them—full speed ahead—that will determine to what extent we prevail.

The imperative to transform education has never been more pressing, and the opportunity to succeed has never been more tangible. The poorest students in our country deserve an opportunity to succeed. We know that teachers matter more than anything else in schools and that by improving teacher quality in the highest-poverty areas we *can* eliminate the student achievement gap and give all children an excellent education. The policy, practice, and research communities are all poised to focus efforts around this task and are currently seeking guidance in how to do so effectively.

This book seeks to support such efforts by providing new insights into how to develop teachers in ways that help them become more effective, improve student learning, and raise the quality of teaching in the areas that need it most. The hope of this book is that readers will take up the charge to capitalize on the many entry points provided by the recent groundswell of support for improving teacher quality—and drive conversations that lead to informed action.

In doing so, we implore you to be bold, be rigorous, and take risks. Be mindful of potential gaps in the road, and create bridges to get you where you need to go. And always remember, the focus of our efforts is to improve student learning, so that all children—regardless of race, origin, gender, language, sexual orientation, ability, or economic circumstances—have the chance to reach their fullest potential.

Notes

Chapter 1

1. William L. Sanders and June C. Rivers, *Cumulative and Residual Effects of Teachers on Future Student Academic Achievement* (Knoxville: University of Tennessee Value-Added Research and Assessment Center, 2000); Linda Darling-Hammond, "Teacher Quality and Student Achievement: A Review of State Policy Evidence," *Education Policy Analysis Archives* 8 (January 2000); S. Rivkin, E. Hanushek, and J. Kain, "Teachers, Schools, and Academic Achievement" (working paper 6691, National Bureau of Economic Research, Cambridge, MA, 1998); Heather Pesky and Katy Haycock, *Teaching Inequality: How Poor and Minority Students Are Short-Changed on Teacher Quality* (Washington, DC: The Education Trust, 2007).

2. Chris Pipho, "The Value Added Side of Standards," *Phi Beta Kappan* (1998): 341–342, http://hub.mspnet.org/index.cfm/9115; Steven Rivken, Eric Hanushek, and John Kain, "Teachers, Schools and Academic Achievement," *Econometrica* 73, no. 2 (2005): 417–458.

3. Robert Gordon, Thomas J. Kane, and Douglas O. Staiger, *Identifying Effective Teachers Using Performance on the Job* (Washington, DC: The Brookings Institution, 2006).

4. Quoted in Jason Snipes and Amanda Horwitz, "Investing in Effective Teachers for High Needs Schools: A Review of Current Research and Practices" (working paper, Ford Foundation, 2007).

5. Jonathan Rochkind et al., *Getting Started: A Survey of New Public School Teachers on Their Training and First Months on the Job* (Washington, DC: National Comprehensive Center for Teacher Quality, 2007).

6. Julien R. Betts, Kim S. Ruben, and Anne Danenberg, *Equal Resources, Equal Outcomes? The Distribution of School Resources and Student Achievement in California* (San Francisco: Public Policy Institute of California, 2000); Eric Hanushek, Steven Rivken, and John Kain, "Why Public Schools Lose Teachers," *Journal of Human Resources* 39 (2004): 326–354; J. Presley, B. White, and Y. Gong, *Examining the Distribution and Impact of Teacher Quality in Illinois* (Chicago: Illinois Education Research Council, 2005).

7. Thomas J. Kane, Jonah E. Rockoff, and Douglas O. Staiger, *Identifying Effective Teachers in New York City* (Cambridge, MA: National Bureau of Economic Research, 2005); R. Murnane and B. R. Phillips, "Learning by Doing, Vintage, and Selection: Three Pieces of the Puzzle Relating to Teaching Experience and Teaching Performance," *Economics of Education Review* 1, no. 4 (1981), 435–465; Steven Rivkin, Eric Hanushek, and John Kain, "Teachers, Schools, and Academic Achievement" (working paper 6691,

National Bureau of Economic Research, Cambridge, MA, 1998); D. Boyd et al., *How Changes in Entry Requirements Alter the Teacher Workforce and Affect Student Achievement* (Albany, NY: Teachers Pathway Project, 2005); National Center for Education Statistics, *Monitoring Quality: An Indicators Report* (Washington, DC: National Center for Education Statistics, 2000).

8. Richard M. Ingersoll, *Is There Really a Teacher Shortage?* (Philadelphia: Consortium for Policy Research in Education, The University of Pennsylvania, 2003).

9. Thomas G. Carroll, *Policy Brief: The High Cost of Teacher Turnover* (Washington, DC: The National Commission on Teaching and America's Future, 2007).

10. New York City Department of Education and Chicago Public Schools teacher populations have consisted of more than 50 percent new teachers, with less than five years teaching experience, in recent years.

11. C. T. Clotfelter, H. F. Ladd, and J. Vigdor, *Who Teaches Whom? Race and the Distribution of Novice Teachers* (Durham, NC: Sanford Institute of Public Policy, Duke University, 2003); Kevin Carey, *The Real Value of Teachers* (Washington, DC: Education Trust, 2004).

12. G. Barnes, E. Crowe, and B. Schaefer, *The Cost of Teacher Turnover in Five School Districts* (Washington, DC: National Commission on Teaching and America's Future, 2007).

13. *Tapping the Potential: Retaining and Developing High Quality Teachers* (Washington, DC: Alliance for Excellence in Education, 2005).

14. Thomas G. Carroll, *Policy Brief: The High Cost of Teacher Turnover* (Washington, DC: The National Commission on Teaching and America's Future (NCTAF), 2007).

15. Elizabeth Whisnant, Kim Elliott, and Susan Pynchon, *A Review of Literature on Beginning Teacher Induction* (Tacoma, WA: The Center for Strengthening the Teaching Profession, July 2005).

16. Robin R. Henke, Xianglei Chen, and Sonya Geis, *Progress Through the Teacher Pipeline: 1992–93 College Graduates and Elementary/Secondary School Teaching as of 1997* (Washington, DC: U.S. Department of Education, National Center for Education Statistics, 2000).

17. D. Goldhaber, B. Gross, and D. Player, "Are Public Schools Really Losing Their 'Best'? Assessing the Career Transitions of Teachers and Their Implication for the Quality of the Teacher Workforce" (working paper 12, Center for Analysis of Longitudinal Data in Education Research, Urban Institute, Washington, DC, 2007).

18. Donald Boyd et al., *How Changes in Entry Requirements Alter the Teacher Workforce and Affect Student Achievement*.

19. U.S. Department of Education, National Center for Education Statistics, *Teacher Follow-Up Survey (Questionnaire for Current Teachers and Questionnaire for Former Teachers), 2004-05* (Washington, DC: Government Printing Office, 2007); MetLife Survey of the American Teacher, *Transitions and the Role of Supportive Relationships: A Survey of Teachers, Principals and Students 2004–05* (New York: MetLife, 2005); Eric Hirsch, Casia Freitas, and Anthony Villar, *Interim Report on Teaching, Learning*

and Leadership Survey Outcomes (Kansas, Massachusetts, West Virginia) (Santa Cruz, CA: New Teacher Center at the University of California at Santa Cruz, 2008).

20. Susan Moore Johnson and Sarah Birkeland, "What Keeps New Teachers in the Swim?" *Journal of Staff Development* 23, no. 4 (Fall 2002): 18–21.

21. Hirsch et al., *Interim Report on Teaching, Learning and Leadership Survey Outcomes (Kansas, Massachusetts, West Virginia).*

22. Richard Ingersoll and Jeff Kralik, *The Impact of Mentoring on Teacher Retention: What the Research Says* (Denver: Education Commission of the States, 2004).

23. Steven Glazerman, Sarah Dolfin, Martha Bleeker, Amy Johnson, Eric Isenberg, Julieta Lugo-Gil, and Mary Grider, Mathematica Policy Research, Inc.; Edward Britton, WestEd; and Melanie Ali, *Impacts of Comprehensive Teacher Induction: Results from the First Year of a Randomized Controlled Study* (Washington, DC: Institute of Education Sciences, October 2008).

24. Although the study's authors screened districts to participate in the study—to avoid including those that had had an experience with "comprehensive induction"—they acknowledge that "it is possible that the screening was imperfect." A possible explanation is that district personnel who confirmed to researchers that their schools had no comprehensive induction support in place may have had insufficient knowledge about individual schools. NTC studies in the Midwest and Hawaii suggest that schools often operate induction programs unknown to district administrators.

25. Debra Viadero, "'No Effects' Studies Raising Eyebrows," *Education Week,* April 1, 2009.

26. Elements from this section have been adapted from the *NTC Response to IES/Mathematica First-Year Report on Teacher Induction,* which can be found at www.newteachercenter.org/pdfs/Mathematica.pdf. Additional thanks to Liam Goldrick for his support in the development of this chapter.

Chapter 2

1. This framework is based on the work of Sharon Feiman-Nemser et al., *A Conceptual Review of Literature on New Teacher Induction* (Washington, DC: National Partnership for Excellence and Accountability in Teaching, 1999).

2. T. M. Smith and R. M. Ingersoll, "What Are the Effects of Induction and Mentoring on Beginning Teacher Turnover?" *American Educational Research Journal* 41, no. 3 (2004): 681–714.

3. Richard M. Ingersoll and Thomas M. Smith, *Do Teacher Induction and Mentoring Matter?* (Alexandria, VA: NASSP Bulletin, 2004).

4. Sanda Balaban, New York City network leader, has coined this phrase to describe the paradigm in which the teaching and learning models provided for students mirror the teaching and learning models provided for teachers, for principals, for deputy chancellors, chancellors, and so on.

5. Jonah Rockoff, "Does Mentoring Reduce Turnover and Improve Skills of New Employees? Evidence from Teachers in New York City," Columbia Business School,

Columbia University, 2008; National Bureau of Economic Research (February 2008), http://ssrn.com/abstract=1147662.

6. Stephen Fletcher and Michael Strong, "A Comparison of Site Based and Full Release Mentoring of Elementary Grade New Teachers: An Analysis of Changes in Student Achievement," submitted for publication.

7. A full-time mentor is likely to observe each week a lesson taught by approximately ten of the fifteen teachers. The mentor does this approximately thirty-five weeks each year, or 350 observed lessons thoughtfully analyzed and assessed with the beginning teacher. A full-release mentor does this for three years, for a total of 1,050 observed and debriefed lessons. Where else in the system do school officials have such potential to develop educational leaders who have deep knowledge of classroom practice and ways to support a teacher's growth?

8. Jeanne Kaufmann, *New and Beginning Teacher Mentoring* (Education Commission of the States, State Notes, Teaching Quality/New Teacher Mentoring, December 2007); Bridget Curran, *Mentoring and Supporting New Teachers* (National Governors Association, NGA Center for Best Practices, January 2002).

9. In the past decade, many states have developed sets of professional teaching standards that attempt to capture the essential knowledge, skills, and dispositions of teaching. Additional examples include the National Board for Professional Teaching Standards Core Propositions, the Interstate New Teacher Support and Assessment Consortium (INTASC) standards, and Charlotte Danielson's Framework for Teaching.

10. K. M. Brown and S. R. Wynn, "Finding, Supporting and Keeping: The Role of the Principal in Teacher Retention Issues," *Leadership and Policy in Schools* 9, no. 1 (January 2009): 37–63; K. Leithwood, K. S. Louis, S. Anderson, and K. Wahlstrom, *Review of Research: How Leadership Influences Student Learning* (New York: The Wallace Foundation, 2004).

11. Over the years, a number of districts have created successful mentoring programs in which the mentors also serve as evaluators of new teachers. These programs require close collaboration between districts and the teacher union or association. The NTC perspective is that linking mentoring to a teacher's ongoing professional growth (not to his evaluation) helps avoid any overtones of compliance and ushers new teachers into an environment of continuous, collaborative learning. Anecdotal data shows that new teachers appreciate having a confidential mentor and are more likely to share challenges or politically sensitive information with a nonevaluative mentor.

12. Anthony S. Bryk and Barbara L. Schneider, *Trust in Schools: A Core Resource for Improvement* (New York: Russell Sage Foundation Publications, 2002).

Chapter 3

1. The developers of the NTC Formative Assessment System and professional development would like to acknowledge the developers, thought leaders, and education pioneers who have influenced the program: Bob Garmston (cognitive coaching); Bena

Kallik (assessment and critical thinking); Marion Diamond (brain research and biology); R. Hanson, H. Silver, and R. Strong (learning styles); Art Costa (critical thinking and thinking skills); Suzanne Bailey (adult learning and group facilitation skills); Pat Wolf (brain-based learning); Grant Wiggins (understanding by design); Linda Lambert (teacher leadership and adult learning); Ann Lieberman (learning from practice); Judith Warren Little (job embedded learning, program teacher expectations, and student achievement). Without their meaningful work to help us understand adult learning, the NTC would not be nearly as successful or powerful in helping mentors move new teacher practice forward.

2. For more on reflective practice, see D. A. Schön, *The Reflective Practitioner: How Professionals Think in Action* (London: Temple Smith, 1983); for more on cognitive coaching, see Robert J. Garmston and Arthur L. Costa, *Cognitive Coaching: A Foundation for Renaissance Schools* (Norwood, MA: Christopher-Gordon, 1994); and for more on Jungian operating and learning styles, see Harvey F. Silver and J. Robert Strong, *Learning Styles and Strategies, 3rd Edition* (Trenton, NJ: Silver, Strong, and Associates, 1996).

3. Rafael Echeverria with Julio Olalla, *The Art of Ontological Coaching, Part One* (San Francisco: The Newfield Group, 1992).

4. Carl D. Glickman, Emily Calhoun, and Jo Roberts, "Clinical Supervision within the School as the Center of Inquiry," in *Clinical Supervision: Coaching for Higher Performance*, ed. Robert H. Anderson and Karolyn J. Snyder (Lanham, MD: ScarecrowEducation, 1996).

5. Ellen Moir, "The Stages of a Teacher's First Year," in *A Better Beginning: Supporting and Mentoring New Teachers,* ed. Marge Scherer (Alexandria, VA: ASCD, 1999), 19–23.

6. D. Berliner, *The Development of Expertise in Pedagogy* (Washington, DC: AACTE Publications, 1988).

7. Members of the New Teacher Center's senior staff led and were involved in the validity study and final development work that resulted in the creation of the California Standards for the Teaching Profession. NTC helped develop the integrated nature of the CSTP and the unique use of indicator questions to articulate classroom practices. These two features serve to breathe life into the CSTP and make the document a useful tool for self-reflection and dialogue.

8. Joseph P. McDonald et al., *The Power of Protocols: An Educator's Guide to Better Practice* (New York: Teachers College Press, 2003).

9. The temptation to mandate use of these tools as forms is great and must be resisted if programs are to use formative assessments for deep learning (as opposed to formative assessments as hoops and hurdles—an outcome NTC has unfortunately seen play out in a number of districts).

10. ASCD, *Another Set of Eyes: Conferencing Skills. Trainer's Manual* (Alexandria, VA: ASCD, 1988); Garmston and Costa, *Cognitive Coaching: A Foundation for Renaissance Schools.*

Chapter 5

1. R. Curtis and S. E. Birkeland, *Ensuring the Support and Development of New Teachers in Boston Public Schools: A Proposal to Address an Urgent Need* (Boston: Boston Public Schools, 2006).

2. Ila Deshmukh Towery, Victoria Hom, and Kenneth Salim, "Hiring (and Keeping) Excellent Urban Teachers: A Coordinated Approach to New Teacher Support" (working paper, Boston Plan for Excellence, 2009).

3. Deshmukh Towery et al., "Hiring (and Keeping) Excellent Urban Teachers: A Coordinated Approach to New Teacher Support."

4. The Boston Teacher Residency program, now a nationally recognized teacher preparation program, rigorously selects candidates, especially candidates of color, and uses a medical-type residency model to place potential candidates in classrooms for thirteen months before they begin their teaching positions.

5. I. Deshmukh Towery et al., "Hiring (and Keeping) Excellent Urban Teachers: A Coordinated Approach to New Teacher Support."

6. Stephen Fletcher and Michael Strong, "A Comparison of Site Based and Full Release Mentoring of Elementary Grade New Teachers: An Analysis of Changes in Student Achievement," submitted for publication, 2008.

7. BPS sought to overcome this obstacle by engaging in a rigorous campaign to support principals in understanding the key elements of selection.

Chapter 6

1. For more information on early program implementation issues, download the New York City policy report: Dara Barlin, *Understanding NYC's Groundbreaking Induction Initiative* (Santa Cruz: New Teacher Center, April 2006), http://newteacher-center.org/nyc_policy_paper.php.

2. Jonah Rockoff, "Does Mentoring Reduce Turnover and Improve Skills of New Employees? Evidence from Teachers in New York City," Columbia Business School, Columbia University, 2008; National Bureau of Economic Research (February 2008), http://ssrn.com/abstract=1147662.

3. Rockoff, "Does Mentoring Reduce Turnover and Improve Skills of New Employees? Evidence from Teachers in New York City."

4. Barlin, *Understanding NYC's Groundbreaking Induction Initiative.*

5. Rockoff, "Does Mentoring Reduce Turnover and Improve Skills of New Employees? Evidence from Teachers in New York City."

Chapter 7

1. ACORN, *Where Have All the Teachers Gone? The Costs of Teacher Turnover in ACORN Neighborhood Schools,* (2003), www.acorn.org/index.php?id=315.

2. Areas are part of the CPS infrastructure to support clusters of schools. They are regional offices and staff, sometimes considered small district offices, that focus pri-

marily on principal supervision, professional development, initiative rollout, and strategic support for a specified number of schools.

Chapter 8

1. The NTC Teaching and Learning Conditions (TLC) Survey is administered every two years across the state of North Carolina and is completed by every teacher and school administrator (greater than 90 percent completion). Former North Carolina governor Mike Easley made such data collection a priority, and current evaluation systems for administrators must include the principal's plan in response to the TLC survey data.

2. A recent study has suggested that this information is critical to successful programs that retain new teachers. See Jonah Rockoff, "Does Mentoring Reduce Turnover and Improve Skills of New Employees? Evidence from Teachers in New York City," Columbia Business School, Columbia University, 2008; National Bureau of Economic Research (February 2008), http://ssrn.com/abstract=1147662.

3. North Carolina's Teacher Working Conditions survey, currently administered by the New Teacher Center, has been conducted in more than a dozen states.

4. In Chicago, schools are divided into twenty-four areas, each with its own administrative team that oversees instruction as well as operational functions in a subset of CPS schools.

5. Rockoff, "Does Mentoring Reduce Turnover and Improve Skills of New Employees? Evidence from Teachers in New York City."

6. The NTC suggests a caseload of no more than fifteen new teachers per fully released mentor and recommends a reduction to twelve or thirteen (or fewer) in urban or low-performing contexts.

7. Arthur Levine, *Educating School Teachers* (The Education Schools Project, September 2006).

Chapter 9

1. Stephen Fletcher and Michael Strong, "A Comparison of Site Based and Full Release Mentoring of Elementary Grade New Teachers: An Analysis of Changes in Student Achievement," submitted for publication, 2008.

About the Authors

Ellen Moir is founder and executive director of the New Teacher Center. For more than twenty years, she has pioneered innovative approaches to new teacher development, research on new teacher practice, and the design and administration of teacher induction programs. Moir has received national recognition for her work, including the 2008 Contribution to the Field Award, the highest honor given by the National Staff Development Council; the Harold W. McGraw, Jr., 2005 Prize in Education; and the 2003 Distinguished Teacher Educator Award from the California Council on Teacher Education.

Dara Barlin is the associate director of policy for the New Teacher Center, assisting state and federal policy makers in developing high-quality induction policies and improved working conditions for educators in our nation's most impoverished areas. She previously served as the education reform program associate at the Ford Foundation, as a research officer at the Institute for Public Policy Research in London, and lead organizer/political consultant for the American Federation of Teachers. Dara presents regularly at education conferences and has coauthored U.S. and international articles focused on teacher retention.

Janet Gless is associate director of the New Teacher Center, where she oversees the center's national teacher induction strategy and program efforts that span forty states as well as a number of international sites. She assists educational organizations, policy makers, administrators, and teacher leaders with the design and implementation of comprehensive teacher induction programs. Prior to cofounding the NTC, Janet served as a visiting educator with the California Department of Education. Janet presents regularly at national and statewide conferences and has coauthored articles and training on new teacher induction.

Jan Miles is northwest regional director at the New Teacher Center. After several years as a mentor and mentor professional developer, Jan now works with state departments of education leadership and induction program leaders across the country and internationally to create robust programs and policies. She is currently directing the NTC MetLife Foundation National Teacher Induction Network, a collaboration of fifteen national programs. As well, she is a regular presenter and speaker at national conferences.

New
Teacher
Center

About the New Teacher Center

The New Teacher Center (NTC) is a national resource dedicated to improving student learning by supporting the development of inspired, dedicated, and highly qualified teachers. Established in 1998, the NTC supports research, policy, and practice related to new teacher mentoring and induction.

The NTC works with school districts, policy makers, and state educational leaders throughout the country to design and implement intensive, mentor-based new teacher and administrator support programs. Since its inception, the New Teacher Center has served more than forty-nine thousand teachers, five thousand mentors, and millions of students in more than forty states and has participated in nearly thirteen hundred contracts with more than three hundred school districts across the country.

In response to the increasing global interest in supporting new teachers, the center has begun working in a number of international communities, including Scotland, New Zealand, Canada, Egypt, and the U.S. territories of Guam and Puerto Rico.

Recognition of the NTC's work includes the following:

NTC Executive Director Ellen Moir was awarded the 2008 Contribution to the Field award, the highest honor given by the National Staff Development Council.

Ellen Moir won the 2005 Harold W. McGraw, Jr., Prize in Education for her dedication to building a national program focused on developing high-quality teacher induction programs.

The U.S. Department of Education featured the Santa Cruz New Teacher Project as an exemplary program at the National Conference on Teacher Quality.

The *Chronicle of Higher Education* called the Santa Cruz New Teacher Project the "gold standard" for induction programs.

Index